Film im Englischunterricht

Gran Torino

Ein Film von Clint Eastwood

Unterrichtsvorschläge und Kopiervorlagen
von Friderike Ulmer

Ernst Klett Sprachen
Stuttgart

Bildnachweis:
21.1 Shutterstock (Everett Historical), New York; 21.2 Shutterstock (Rainer Lesniewski), New York; 21.2 Klett-Archiv (Maja Merz), Stuttgart; 22.1 Shutterstock (Lissandra Melo), New York; 22.2 Shutterstock (Mirec), New York; 22.2 Klett-Archiv (Maja Merz), Stuttgart; 23 Friderike Ulmer, Tübingen; 30 Shutterstock (Rachata Teyparsit), New York; 33 Klett-Archiv (Maja Merz), Stuttgart; 33 Shutterstock (AVA Bitter), New York; 35 123RF.com (Andrea Crisante), Nidderau; 37 Cedric Weber / Shutterstock, Inc; 38 Shutterstock (Uncle Leo), New York; 40 Thinkstock (Wavebreakmedia Ltd), München; 60 Shutterstock (Sakurra), New York; 70 Friderike Ulmer, Tübingen; 80 Shutterstock (Maximus256), New York

1. Auflage   1 ⁸ ⁷ ⁶ ⁵ ⁴ | 2024 23 22 21 20

Alle Drucke dieser Auflage sind unverändert und können im Unterricht nebeneinander verwendet werden.
Die letzte Zahl bezeichnet das Jahr des Druckes.

www.klett-sprachen.de

Autorin: Friderike Ulmer
Redaktion: Paul Newcomb
Zeichnerin: Maja Merz
Layoutkonzeption: Elmar Feuerbach, Sandra Vrabec
Gestaltung und Satz: bostext, Friolzheim
Umschlaggestaltung: Maja Merz
Titelbild: Shutterstock (Panacea Doll), New York, NY
Druck und Bindung: CEWE Stiftung & Co. KGaA, Germering

Printed in Germany

ISBN 978-3-12-577484-1

Inhaltsverzeichnis

Vorwort und Einleitung – Wichtige Hinweise!

Der Film

Gran Torino (2008) ist die 29. Produktion des Altmeisters Clint Eastwood, der in diesem Spielfilm nicht nur die Regie führt und die Hauptrolle des Walt Kowalski spielt, sondern selbst den Abschlusssong mit komponiert und gesungen hat. *Gran Torino* ist Drama, psychologischer Thriller, Actionfilm und urbaner Western und belegt bei den IMDb Charts immerhin den 157. Platz unter den 250 Top-Rated Movies der Online-Filmdatenbank.

http://www.imdb.com/
chart/top
(Stand: Januar 2016)

Gran Torino hat großes Potential eine Bandbreite von SuS zu motivieren, da er durch seine Mischung aus spannenden, komischen und tragischen Momenten gute Unterhaltung bietet, seine lineare Erzählstruktur ihn leicht verständlich macht und seine politisch inkorrekte Sprache eine willkommene Abwechslung zu den gewohnten Texten bietet. Was ihn darüber hinaus für den Unterricht interessant macht, ist, dass er als „kultureller Ausdrucksträger" gesehen werden kann, in dem sich Glaubensgrundsätze, Wertvorstellungen und Auffassungsweisen einer Kultur widerspiegeln. Wie alle anderen Eastwood Filme zeigt Gran Torino „an urgent engagement with the tougher, messier, bigger questions of American life": Rassimus, Vorurteile und Toleranz, Waffengewalt im Krieg und im Vorgarten, Individualismus und Männlichkeit. In *Clint Eastwood's America* betont Sam B. Girgus zudem die ethisch-moralische Dimension der Filme: „Eastwood as a serious director and as an American artist injects a moral and ethical sensibility into his work, a sensibility imbued with the dilemmas and challenges of modernity and the American imagination."

Henseler, Roswitha et al.
(2011). Filme im Englischunterricht. Grundlagen,
Methoden, Genres. Klett/
Kallmeyer. S. 10

www.nytimes.com

Sam B. Girgus (2014).
Clint Eastwood's America
(America through the lens).
Polity Press. S. 13

Die mannigfachen kontroversen Themen des Films laden ein zum Recherchieren, Analysieren, Diskutieren und Vergleichen. Dabei ist eine filmimmanente Betrachtungsweise ebenso lohnenswert wie eine Einbettung in den landeskundlichen Kontext des Films.

Das Konzept: Zwei Hauptmodule

Ab dem Abitur 2019 ist *Gran Torino* in Baden-Württemberg Teil des Pflichtkanons des Schwerpunktthemas *The Ambiguity of Belonging*. Es wäre jedoch schade, den Film nur durch diese thematische Brille zu betrachten, denn er bietet ein sehr viel breiteres Spektrum an spannenden und unterrichtsrelevanten Aspekten. Für dieses Filmheft wurden deshalb zwei unterschiedliche Module für die Auseinandersetzung mit dem Film konzipiert, die unabhängig voneinander einsetzbar sind. Während Kapitel 1 (*Hinführung zum Film*) als Pflichtmodul gesehen werden soll, können bei Kapitel 2: (*Filmarbeit*) entweder Modul A oder Modul B (etwa 10 Schulstunden pro Modul) oder – falls genügend Zeit zur Verfügung steht – Modul A und Modul B unterrichtet werden. Sehr gut durchführbar ist auch eine Kombination aus beiden Modulen: Modul A und einzelne Aufgaben aus Modul B, bzw. Modul B und einzelne Aufgaben aus Modul A. Unter *Organisation und Ablauf* wird im jeweiligen Modul explizit auf Kombinationsmöglichkeiten hingewiesen. (Siehe zum Beispiel Modul (2)B auf Seite 51).

Modul A nähert sich dem Film in seiner thematischen Breite und beleuchtet arbeitsteilig fünf verschiedene Themen: *Prejudices and Racism, Masculinity, Gran Torino* (the car), *Violence* und *Religion*. Nach der gemeinsamen Hinführung (Kapitel 1) setzen sich die SuS in Projektgruppen („theme groups") eigenständig mit einem der genannten Themen auseinander. Dabei stehen klar strukturierte und motivierend konzipierte Arbeitsblätter zur Verfügung. Ihre Arbeitsergebnisse stellen alle Themengruppen abschließend anhand einer selbst gewählten Filmszene vor. Die Präsentationen können zur mündlichen Leistungsüberprüfung herangezogen werden.

Das Thema *The Ambiguity of Belonging* – im Deutschen vielleicht am besten übersetzt mit „Nicht-wissen-wo-man-hingehört" – ist für SuS aufgrund seiner Offenheit und Vielschichtigkeit zunächst nicht unbedingt leicht greifbar. Deswegen führt **Modul B** inhaltlich und sprachlich ins Thema ein, bevor sich die SuS mithilfe abwechslungsreich gestalteter Arbeitsblätter zu sieben ausgewählten Szenen vertieft mit dem Film beschäftigen. Es werden sowohl das Hörsehverstehen als auch das Leseverstehen geschult und ein vertieftes Textverständnis durch formalästhetische und kreative Aufgabenstellungen gefördert. Als Vorschlag zur Leistungsmessung steht eine Klausur zur Auswahl, welche an die Aufgabenformate des Abiturs angelehnt ist und die im Modul erarbeiteten Inhalte, sprachlichen Strukturen und Kompetenzen überprüft.

In Kapitel 1 (*Hinführung zum Film*) gibt es zudem Materialien und Aufgaben-stellungen zur Einführung in die Filmanalyse, Pre-viewing Activities zum Film und Sachtexte zum landeskundlichen Hintergrund, die auf beide Module zugeschnitten sind.

Unabhängig vom Modul empfiehlt sich zunächst eine **Präsentation des Spielfilms *en bloc***, die durch eine dem Modul angepasste While-viewing Aufgabe begleitet wird. Die Sichtung kann je nach Verfügbarkeit im Unterricht oder zuhause erfolgen. Rückmeldungen von SuS belegen, dass diese natürliche Form des Filmeschauens die Motivation für die anschließende Detailanalyse einzelner Szenen entscheidend steigert. Die Aufgabenstellungen im Modul B eignen sich jedoch ebenso für eine step-by-step Sichtung und Erarbeitung.

Alle gegebenen Zeitangaben in diesem Filmheft beziehen sich auf die DVD Version von *Gran Torino*, nicht etwa andere Online-Versionen (Amazon usw).

Klett Online-Links

Mit diesem Lehrerhandbuch bekommen Sie Zugriff auf Zusatzmaterialien im Internet, die durch einen **Online-Link** im Text gekennzeichnet sind. Geben Sie den Code in das Suchfeld auf www.klett-sprachen.de ein und Sie werden direkt auf die zutreffenden Internet-Links verwiesen.

Die methodisch-didaktischen Schwerpunkte

- Förderung der interkulturellen kommunikativen Kompetenz und des Fremd-verstehens durch Aneignung soziokulturellen Wissens, durch die Identifikation mit Charakteren einer anderen Lebenswelt und durch den Vergleich fremder Kulturen mit der eigenen Kultur.
- Konsequente Lernerorientierung durch Materialien/Aufgaben, welche die SuS emotional involvieren und zum interaktiven Agieren in der Zielsprache auffordern.
- Sinnvolle Sprechanlässe mit dem Partner, in der Gruppe oder im Plenum, die zu möglichst lebensweltlichen Kommunikationssituationen führen (sich auf etwas einigen, Informationen austauschen, Grafiken versprachlichen und erläutern, Vergleiche ziehen, unterschiedliche Ergebnisse und Meinungen austauschen und auswerten).
- Schüleraktivierende Aufgabenorientierung (Modul B), die das eigenverant-wortliche Lernen fördert und ein authentisches Sprachhandeln zum Ziel hat.
- Unterschiedliche Formen der integrierten Spracharbeit, die vor allem den thematischen Wortschatz der SuS um Kollokationen und idiomatische Ausdrücke erweitern und ein Bewusstsein für unterschiedliche Register und deren Bedeutung für interkulturelle Begegnungen schaffen.
- Verbindliche und herausfordernde Aufgabenstellungen mit sinnvollem *Scaffolding* und klarer Zielorientierung, welche für einen sprachlichen, inhaltlichen und methodischen Lernzuwachs der SuS sorgen und dem Niveau der Oberstufe gerecht werden.
- Unterschiedliche Differenzierungsangebote: Zusatzaufgaben für besonders schnelle und leistungsstarke SuS, unterschiedliche Themen, die zur Auswahl stehen, großes Methoden- und Aufgabenspektrum, das analytische, kreative, visuelle und kinästhetische Lerntypen anspricht.

Das begleitende Schülerarbeitsheft für SuS

Begleitend zu diesem Lehrerhandbuch gibt es ein Arbeitsheft für SuS (Klett-Nr.: 577485), das aus einer kurzen Einleitung mit Tipps für die Bearbeitung von Filmen, der Synopse sowie allen Arbeitsblättern aus diesem Lehrerhandbuch besteht. Im Schülerbuch finden sich ebenfalls die Lösungsvorschläge zu den *Language Sheets* aus beiden Modulen (KV A1.L – A5.L und KB B5).

Abkürzungen/Abbreviations

EA	Einzelarbeit	KV	Kopiervorlage
ES	Ergebnissicherung	L	Lehrkraft
e.g.	exempli gratia (for example)	PA	Partnerarbeit
HA	Hausaufgaben	S	Schülerin/Schüler
i.e.	id est (that is)	SuS	Schülerinnen und Schüler
		TPS	Think-Pair-Share
		UG	Unterrichtsgespräch

Gran Torino: Synopse des Films

Setting: Detroit, state of Michigan, USA. Walt Kowalski's house is in Highland Park, a neighborhood in the north of the former 'Motor City'.

Chapter/ running time	Summary	Quotes
Chapter 1 00:00:00 – 00:03:43	[Opening credits/theme tune *Gran Torino*] Dorothy Kowalski's funeral At his wife's funeral Walt Kowalski shows contempt for both the shallow sermon of Father Janovich, and his own sons and grandchildren, who behave in a disrespectful and self-absorbed way.	"Don't you think he'll get in trouble by himself in the old neighborhood?" "He's still living in the 50s."
2 00:03:44 – 00:08:22	**Walt's family and neighbors** At the funeral reception at his house, Walt can hardly bear the people around him: His grandsons sneak around in his basement and find a box full of mementos from Walt's time as soldier in the Korean War, among them a Silver Star medal. Meanwhile his Asian neighbors are having a party with many guests. Walt's teenage granddaughter Ashley discovers his immaculate Gran Torino in his garage and wonders if she could inherit it. The shy Hmong teenager from next door, Thao Van Lor, disturbs the reception asking if he can borrow a starter cable and is rudely sent away. The priest asks Walt to come to confession, because Dorothy had wanted it. Walt outspokenly refuses to do so.	"How many swamp rats can you get in one room?"
3 00:08:23 – 00:12:39	**Thao and his family** The Hmong guests are arriving when Walt's guests are leaving. The family is celebrating the birth of a baby with traditional rituals. Thao has problems fitting in. Father Janovich makes another attempt to approach Walt and is kicked out once again.	"How can he ever become the man of the house?"
4 00:12:40 – 00:17:21	**Thao's initiation** Thao is bullied by members of a Hispanic gang driving by in a car. Thao's older cousin Spider and his friends see this happening and chase them away. In return they expect Thao to join their gang. Thao refuses at first but is finally willing to undergo an initiation test: stealing Walt's prized car, a 1972 Gran Torino Sport.	"Is you a girl or is you a boy, man? I can't tell."
5 00:17:22 – 00:20:03	**Locals at the bar** Walt is telling racist jokes in a bar when the persistent Father Janovich shows up and talks Walt into chatting about life and death. They have a beer and Walt actually opens up and shares some of his haunting memories of the battlefields in Korea.	"Sounds like you know a lot more about death than you do living!"
6 00:20:04 – 00:23:19	**Thao's crime [theme tune 'Gran Torino'].** Late at night, Walt thwarts Thao's attempt to steal the Gran Torino. The boy only gets away because Walt falls and hurts himself. The next day Walt's son Mitch calls, pretending to ask only how his father is, the real reason is he wants season tickets for football. In the evening, Walt polishes his immaculate Gran Torino in the driveway before proudly admiring it from his porch.	"Ain't she sweet."
7 00:23:20 – 00:27:36	**Walt saves Thao** At night Spider and his gang show up at Thao's house and try to force him to get in their car with them. Sue stands up to them verbally, but the conflict quickly turns into a violent fight between Thao's family and the gang. Then Walt suddenly shows up and chases the intruders away with his rifle – the same weapon with which he had shot a teenage boy in the Korean War. The next day Walt finds his porch full of presents. The Hmong see him as community hero because he saved Thao. Sue introduces her family, undaunted by Walt's insolent behavior. Thao apologizes for trying to steal the Gran Torino but Walt only warns him to never set foot on his property again.	"Get off my lawn."

Chapter/ running time	Summary	Quotes
8 00:27:37 – 00:30:21	**Walt and the priest** Hearing about the fight the night before, Father Janovich visits Walt. He is upset that Walt didn't call the police. He begs him to go to confession, saying it will release him from past burdens. Walt does not want to go, but shows more respect for the priest.	"The thing that haunts a man most is what he isn't ordered to do."
9 00:30:22 – 00:34:47	**Walt saves Sue** Sue and her white date Trey get into trouble with three black teenagers on the sidewalk. They start sexually harassing Sue, who courageously defends herself verbally. Walt happens to pass by in his car and intervenes after observing the scene. The gang only let Sue go after Walt pulls his pistol. Walt sends Trey off and gives Sue a ride home.	"These guys don't want to be your bro and I don't blame them."
10 00:34:48 – 00:38:33	**Sue and Walt in the truck** In the truck Sue explains to Walt who the Hmong are and why Thao appears to be so weak. Later, while reading the newspaper on his porch, Walt is positively surprised when he observes how Thao helps an elderly lady with her grocery bags.	"He [Thao] just doesn't know which direction to go in."
11 00:38:34 – 00:41:56	**Walt's birthday** Mitch and his wife Karen visit Walt on his birthday – as it turns out only to try to persuade him to leave the house and live in a senior's retirement home. They get kicked out. Walt celebrates his birthday alone on his porch. Sue shows up as he has just emptied his last beer can and convinces him to join the Hmong barbecue next door.	- "Just keep your hands off my dog." - "No worries. We only eat cats."
12 00:41:57 – 00:46:42	**The Hmong party** Walt feels uncomfortable among the Hmong until Sue introduces him to their code of behavior and he gets to enjoy their delicious food. Walt is disturbed when the Hmong shaman "reads him", accurately analyzing his life in only a few sentences. Sue is truly worried about Walt when she sees him coughing blood.	"I have more in common with these gooks than I do (with) my own rotten family."
13 00:46:43 – 00:51:41	**Walt's lecture** Finally Walt enjoys being surrounded by the Hmong ladies flattering and spoiling him with lots of food. Then Sue takes him downstairs to the basement, where the young Hmong are hanging out. Thao is sitting unhappily in a corner of the room. Walt rudely tells him off for not asking Youa, a good looking Hmong girl who is apparently interested in Thao, for a date.	"I never thought you were worse with women than you are at stealing cars."
14 00:51:42 – 00:54:42	**Thao's amends** Thao's family insists on Thao making up for trying to steal the Gran Torino. He is to work for Walt to pay his debt. On the first day, Walt makes Thao count the birds in the tree.	"You just go over there and count the birds."
15 00:54:43 – 00:58:33	**Thao's formation** From the second day on, Walt really sets Thao to work. He makes him fix the dilapidated house across the street. Thao works very hard all week, cleaning up the neighborhood [theme tune: 'Gran Torino']. Walt's coughing gets worse.	"You want me to watch paint dry?"
16 00:58:34 – 01:01:41	**Walt's diagnosis** Walt is irritated because he is no longer to be treated by his (presumably) white male doctor, Dr. Feldman, but by a young female Asian, Dr. Chu. Walt calls his son Mitch to tell him about his fatal diagnosis. Mitch, however, is so self-absorbed that he doesn't realize what his father is telling him [theme tune: 'Gran Torino']. From his porch, Walt observes how Spider and the gang still don't leave Thao alone.	"This kid doesn't have a chance."

Chapter/ running time	Summary	Quotes
17 01:01:42 – 01:07:47	**Mutual support** Thao asks Walt to help him fix a faucet in the kitchen. When Walt sees that Thao really would like to fix their rundown house he gives him some tools. In his garage Walt finds out that Thao only tried to steal the Gran Torino because he had been under pressure from the Hmong gang. Thao is concerned when he witnesses Walt coughing up blood. Then Walt asks for Thao's help to carry a freezer up the stairs from the basement. Sue comments on the irony that Walt lets Thao wash the car he had tried to steal from him and thanks him for looking after her brother, who doesn't have a father.	Sue: "He [Thao] doesn't have any real role models in his life."
18 01:07:48 – 01:13:18	**Manning up Thao** While Thao is working in Walt's garden they talk about Walt's life – his job as an assembly worker for Ford, his army service, his son's job, his illness – and about Thao's future. Walt offers to "man Thao up", get him a job and a date with Youa. He sees manliness at the barber shop: Walt and his friend try to teach him "how real men talk".	"Of course I have to make a little adjustment and man you up a little bit."
19 01:13:19 – 01:16:46	**Thao's job** Walt uses his connections to get Thao a job at a construction site, where Thao can prove that he has learned the language of real men. At a hardware store they buy a tool belt and some basics for Thao's new job. Thao thanks Walt for his support.	"What do you wanna do? Carry your tools in a rice bag?"
20 01:16:47 – 01:19:29	**The assault** On his way home, Thao is attacked by his cousin's gang. He bravely tries to defend himself but has no chance against five men. He tries to hide the assault as some of Walt's tools got broken. When Walt finds out a few days later, he wants revenge.	"Cowards!"
21 01:19:30 – 01:22:40	**Walt's revenge** Walt drives up to the gang's house and beats up Smokey, second in command in the gang, threatens him with a gun, warning him to leave Thao alone. Next day Walt has Thao, Sue, their mother and Youa over for a BBQ in his backyard. When he finds out that Thao has asked Youa out on a date, he asks him if he wants to take the Gran Torino.	"If I have to come back here, it's gonna get fucking ugly."
22 01:22:41 – 01:25:34	**The gang's retaliation** While Walt is watching TV at home one night, the Hmong gang drives by and shoots up Thao's home with machine guns. Walt goes over. Thao has been injured slightly, but Sue is missing. Sitting at the table waiting for Sue, Walt questions his act of vendetta. When Sue finally turns up, raped and badly beaten, Walt is devastated and leaves.	"In the war, we just lost a lot of friends, but you're kind of set for it."
23 01:25:35 – 01:29:38	**Walt's reaction** In the darkness of his house, Walt blames himself. He smashes the glass doors of his kitchen cabinet with his knuckles. Father Janovich comes in to find out what Walt is going to do. Drinking a can of beer in the darkness of the room, they talk openly. It becomes clear that Walt feels he has to destroy the gang.	"You know, Thao and Sue are never gonna find peace in this world."
24 01:29:39 – 01:32:33	**Walt's preparations** In the morning, Thao enters Walt's house, agitated. He demands immediate action but Walt manages to calm him down and make him wait until the afternoon. Walt mows his lawn, takes a bath, gets a hair cut and a straight shave at the barber's and buys a fitted suit, something he has never done in his life.	"Now is the time to stay calm."

Chapter/ running time	Summary	Quotes
25 01:32:34 – 01:34:37	**Walt's confession** Dressed up in his new suit, Walt goes to see Father Janovich. When Walt says he wants to make a confession, the priest fears that he has killed someone or plans to do so. It turns out that Walt's worst sin was that he was never close to his sons. The priest absolves him of his sin and tries to find out his plan, urging him to not seek vengeance.	The Father and Walt "Go in peace." "Oh, I am at peace."
26 01:34:38 – 01:39:29	**Walt gearing up** Walt is cleaning his rifle in the kitchen when Thao shows up at the appointed time. Thao is eager to kill the gang although he has never used a weapon in his life. Walt takes Thao to his basement to give him his Silver Star, a medal he earned in Korea, where Walt killed at least 13 people. Then he locks Thao up in the basement to take revenge alone. He confesses to killing an innocent, teenage soldier. Walt wants to prevent Thao from carrying such a haunting burden, too. Walt calls Thao his friend. Thao is outraged as Walt leaves. Father Janovich and the two police officers who have been watching Smokie's house for hours get orders to leave. Father Janovic had obviously alerted the police that Walt might show up seeking retribution. Sue finally hears Thao's shouting and sets him free. He runs to Smokie's house, Sue follows him.	"I got blood on my soul. I'm soiled."
27 01:39:30 – 01:41:46	**Walt's ruse** Walt is standing still in front of Smokie's house. He is patiently waiting until the Hmong thugs notice him through the half-open blinds and step out onto the porch. Walt condemns them for their crime: raping a girl from their own family. Alerted by the noise, many neighbors witness the scene. The "miniature cowboys", as Walt calls them, pull their guns when Walt gets a cigarette out of his outer jacket pocket. With his hand he gestures to shoot them, his index finger pointing at each one of them. Then he reaches slowly into his inside jacket pocket – it looks like he is about to pull a gun. He is immediately brutally executed by deafening bursts of automatic gunfire. He falls backwards onto the ground and lies there, his arms spread like Jesus on the Cross. His right hand opens to reveal not a gun, but his 1st Division Cavalry Zippo lighter, covered in blood.	"Me I've got a light"
28 01:41:47 – 01:46:29	**Justice** [theme tune: 'Gran Torino'] Walt is lying on the ground, almost peacefully, when the police show up. When Thao and Sue arrive in the Gran Torino, a Hmong officer tells them what happened, and that the gang will now be put in jail for a long time. Thao, Sue (her face still terribly bruised) and Father Janovich watch Walt being carried into a vehicle and the gang members being led away by the police. Probably a few days later, Thao, Sue and their mother leave their house in traditional Hmong clothes to go to Walt's funeral. In church, Walt's family is looking skeptically at the Hmong people across the aisle. Father Janovich's sermon reveals his close relationship to Walt and his deep admiration for him. Later Walt's family and Thao sit together at the lawyer's office where Walt's will is being read out. To the family's surprise and disappointment, the house goes to the Church and the Gran Torino to his friend Thao [theme tune: 'Gran Torino']. This scene fades into Thao driving his new car with Daisy the dog by his side.	"These guys will be locked up for a long time."
29 01:46:30–51:47	Thao is driving along the shore of Lake Saint Claire. [credits]	"Gentle now a tender breeze blows"

I   Hinführung zum Film (KV 1 bis 8)

Unabhängig davon, ob Sie Modul A oder Modul B (oder beide) unterrichten möchten, empfiehlt sich vor der intensiven inhaltlichen, filmästhetischen und sprachlichen Auseinandersetzung mit *Gran Torino* eine Hinführung zum Film, welche die SuS vorab gezielt informiert, sensibilisiert und motiviert.

Konzept dieses in die Welt des Films einführenden Moduls

Falls es sich um die erste Filmeinheit im Schuljahr handelt, bietet sich zudem eine allgemeine Hinführung zum Thema Film in Form einer Speaking Activity an (KV 1). Anschließend kann es – abhängig vom Vorwissen und den Vorerfahrungen der SuS – erforderlich sein, eine kurze methodische und sprachliche Einführung in die Filmanalyse einzuschieben (KV 2).

Beide Unterrichtsmodule im Kapitel 2 setzen voraus, dass die SuS mit den Grundbegriffen der Filmanalyse vertraut sind und über einen reichhaltigen Wortschatz der "language of film" verfügen. Hierzu dienen sowohl die *Film terminology* (KV 2), als auch drei weitere optionale Worksheets, die über

Download über Online-Link: zkdgvtu

www.klett-sprachen.de als kostenlose Downloads erhältlich sind (Code: zkdgvtu ins Suchfeld eingeben, Enter drücken: „Describing the film and the film world")

Das Heft bietet danach drei Pre-viewing Activities zur Auswahl, welche die SuS inhaltlich und sprachlich auf den Film einstimmen und den Blick bereits auf Aspekte lenken, die im Laufe der Einheit vertieft betrachtet werden (KV 3–5). Um das Verständnis des Films in seiner historischen und kulturellen Bedingtheit zu erleichtern, stehen zudem drei Texte zur Verfügung, die den SuS wichtige Hintergrundinformationen vermitteln (KV 6–8).

Die Lösungshinweise zu diesen Arbeitsblättern finden Sie im Anhang (Kapitel 3) des Heftes ab Seite 92.

Allgemeine Hinführung zur Filmarbeit

Als Auftakt zur Filmeinheit eignet sich eine Speaking Activity, bei der die SuS ihre eigenen Gewohnheiten, Meinungen und Ideen zum Thema Film zum Ausdruck bringen können (KV 1). Diese KV ist nicht im Schülerbuch enthalten!

Lernziel: SuS können ein Gespräch über persönliche Vorlieben, Vorerfahrungen und Vorwissen zum Thema Film führen, auf unterschiedliche Gesprächspartner eingehen und ihre eigenen Vorstellungen mit denen anderer vergleichen.

Material: Impulsfragen auf Papierstreifen (KV 1)

Sozialform: Speed Dating/Partnerarbeit, zusammenführendes Unterrichtsgespräch.

Ablauf: Die Lehrkraft schneidet die Kopien der Vorlage in Streifen und legt jeweils 3–4 unterschiedliche Impulsfragen auf einen Zweiertisch. Die SuS tauschen sich über eine oder mehrere der ausliegenden Fragen aus und wechseln auf ein Signal der Lehrkraft hin zwei bis drei Mal den Gesprächspartner. Die Zettel bleiben dabei auf den Tischen liegen. Als Alternative zu dieser bewegten Form kann die Aufgabe auch mit mehr Impulsfragen in herkömmlicher Partnerarbeit durchgeführt werden. Eine abschließende Reflexion der Ergebnisse kann im Unterrichtsgespräch folgen.

Einführung in die Filmanalyse

Für Klassen und Kurse, die noch über keine Grundkenntnisse der Filmanalyse verfügen, kann vorab eine kurze Einführung in die wichtigsten Grundkonzepte und -begriffe der Filmanalyse erfolgen. Das Lernen und die Anwendung der Terminologie soll keinen Selbstzweck erfüllen, sondern lediglich als Handwerkszeug für die Auseinandersetzung mit dem Film dienen. Die Einführung erfolgt in drei Schritten: 1. Begriffsklärung „Cinematography" durch einen kurzen Videoclip, 2. Erlernen der Terminologie mithilfe eines Arbeitsblattes, 3. Anwendung der Terminologie anhand eines Filmausschnitts.

Lernziel: SuS können den Begriff *cinematography* erklären. Sie können unterschiedliche Filmtechniken einer Filmsequenz differenziert beschreiben und deren Wirkung interpretieren.

Material: YouTube Video (5:45 min) (*Cinematography 101: What is Cinematography?* unter Online-Link, Code: emnmw2x), KV 2, ein beliebiger bekannter Filmausschnitt oder Kurzfilm (z. B. "Pizza Verdi" (8 min), frei verfügbar auf dem Videoportal Vimeo)

Sozialform: Einzelarbeit, Unterrichtsgespräch

Ablauf: Der Titel des Clips beinhaltet die Frage, welche die SuS während der Sichtung des kurzen Clips stichwortartig schriftlich beantworten sollen. Die Ergebnisse werden zentral gesichert (z. B.: *Cinematography is the art and technology of visual storytelling. In order to communicate with the viewer, filmmakers use a „language of film", which – just like any other language – relies on rules and conventions. It is a language that everybody understands, since specific cinematic techniques have certain effects on people and convey certain emotions*).

Online-Link über klett-sprachen.de: emnmw2x

Im Anschluss lernen die SuS mithilfe eines Arbeitsblattes zentrale Kategorien und Begriffe der Filmanalyse kennen (KV 2). In einem letzten Schritt wenden die SuS die neu erlernten Begriffe an und analysieren Funktion und Wirkungskraft einzelner Filmtechniken. Dazu kann ein beliebiger Filmausschnitt gewählt werden. Sie SuS sollten bereits inhaltlich mit dem Film vertraut sein, um ihre Aufmerksamkeit ganz auf formalästhetische Aspekte lenken zu können. Der Ausschnitt wird abgespielt und von der Lehrkraft an beliebigen Stellen gestoppt, sodass der jeweilige Screenshot beschrieben, die Funktion der Einstellung analysiert und der Effekt auf den Zuschauer interpretiert werden können. Alternativ können die SuS selbst das Signal zum Anhalten des Films geben, wenn sie eine interessante Einstellung sehen. Sehr empfehlenswert ist hierfür der preisgekrönte Kurzfilm „Pizza Verdi" (2012), der auch thematisch zu Gran Torino passt: Bei dem knapp 8-minütigen Kurzfilm geht es um Vorurteile und Voreingenommenheit.

Die Vokabelblätter (*Describing films and the film world*, Downloads, siehe oben) liefern zusätzlich differenzierten Wortschatz zur Beschreibung und Analyse von Filmen und stellen eine sprachliche Unterstützung für beide Module dar.

Pre-viewing activities (KV 3 bis 5)

Die drei vorgeschlagenen Pre-viewing Activities können grundsätzlich für beide Module eingesetzt werden. Die erste Option (KV 3, *Movie trailer*) lenkt jedoch die Aufmerksamkeit auf die Konflikte zwischen den Figuren und Figurengruppen und eignet sich besonders zur Hinführung auf das Thema des Modul B, *The Ambiguity of Belonging*. Die beiden anderen Optionen (KV 4, *Movie poster* und KV 5, *Speed viewing*) führen auf Aspekte hin, die z.T. in Modul A erarbeitet werden. Da Zielsetzungen, Material und Aufgabenstellung aller drei Pre-viewing Activities unterschiedlich sind, ist es auch denkbar, mehrere Optionen zu kombinieren.

Movie Trailer (KV 3)

Lernziel: SuS erweitern ihren Wortschatz zur Beschreibung und Bewertung eines Films. Sie können aus einem Trailer Konflikte zwischen Personen oder Personengruppen herauslesen und beschreiben. Sie können Vermutungen über zentrale Themen des Films anstellen, indem sie einen alternativen Titel formulieren.

Material: Original-Trailer (auf DVD, oder Online, beispielsweise über Klett Online-Link a377652) und KV 3.

Trailer über Online-Link a377652

Sozialform: Think – Pair – Share (zusammenführendes Unterrichtsgespräch)

Ablauf: Um Task 1 bearbeiten zu können, benötigen die SuS ggf. die Hilfe der Lehrkraft zur Klärung unbekannter Wörter oder ein Wörterbuch. Die Ergebnissicherung kann exemplarisch erfolgen. Wegen der Schnelligkeit der Bilder und Schnitte wird der Trailer im Normalfall zwei Mal gezeigt. Beim ersten Mal geben die SuS lediglich eine allgemeine persönliche Einschätzung ab, indem sie aus der Liste Adjektive auswählen, die ihrer Meinung nach auf den Film zutreffen bzw. nicht zutreffen. Bei Task 3 deuten die SuS Bilder und Sprache, um mögliche Konflikte zwischen den unterschiedlichen Parteien zu erkennen. Sie visualisieren ihre Beobachtungen in einer vorstrukturierten Grafik und versprachlichen diese anschließend im Austausch mit dem Partner oder im Plenum.

Movie Poster (KV 4)

Lernziel: SuS können Komposition und Kontraste eines Filmposters erkennen, beschreiben und Deutungsversuche anstellen. Sie können Vermutungen über die Gattung und mögliche Themen des Films zum Ausdruck bringen.

Material: Original-Filmposter (→ Google: "Gran Torino movie poster"), KV 4

Sozialform: Think – Pair – Share (zusammenführendes Unterrichtsgespräch)

Ablauf: Für Task 1 wird das Poster zentral projiziert. Die Ergebnisse werden zunächst mit dem Partner verglichen und diskutiert und abschließend in einem Unterrichtsgespräch gebündelt. Für Task 2 bietet sich eine ähnliche Vorgehensweise an.

Speed Viewing (KV 5)

Technischer Hinweis: Überprüfen Sie, ob die Schnellvorlauf- und Schnellrücklauffunktion auf Ihrem Abspielgerät funktioniert!

Lernziel: SuS erweitern ihren Wortschatz zur Benennung universeller Themen. Sie können auf der Basis eines Schnelldurchlaufs der ersten Hälfte des Films Vorhersagen über zentrale Themen des Films anstellen. Bei einem zweiten Schnelldurchlauf können die SuS typische Momente der amerikanischen Kultur im Film identifizieren und die Symbolik bekannter Ikonen beschreiben und Verbindungen zu universellen Themen herstellen. Aufgrund ihrer Beobachtungen können die SuS einen alternativen Filmtitel formulieren.

Material: Film und KV 5

Sozialform: Think – Pair – Share (zusammenführendes Unterrichtsgespräch)

Ablauf: Um Task 1 bearbeiten zu können, benötigen die SuS ggf. die Hilfe der Lehrkraft zur Klärung unbekannter Wörter oder ein Wörterbuch. Eine Zusammenführung der Ergebnisse dieser Task im Plenum ist nur auf Wunsch der SuS empfehlenswert, da die Aufgabenstellung sehr persönlich ist. Die Ergebnissicherungen von Tasks 3 und 4 können ggf. direkt im Plenum erfolgen.

Historischer und kultureller Hintergrund

Korean War/The Hmong and the „Secret War" (KV 6 und KV 7)

Ein zumindest grobes Wissen über Amerikas militärische Intervention in Korea und die Geschichte der Hmong in der zweiten Hälfte des 20. Jahrhunderts sind für das Verständnis des Films unabdingbar. Hierfür stehen zwei Texte mit kommunikativer Aufgabenstellung zur Verfügung.

Lernziel: SuS können einem Sachtext Informationen entnehmen und mit deren Hilfe eine Grafik beschreiben und erläutern. Sie können den Inhalt ihres eigenen Textes mit dem ihres Partners in Verbindung setzen.
Material: Zwei kurze Texte mit Grafiken (KV 6 und KV 7)
Sozialform: Einzelarbeit, Partnerarbeit, abschließendes Unterrichtsgespräch
Ablauf: Es bilden sich Paare, die zunächst arbeitsteilig beide Texte in Einzelarbeit lesen und sich durch Markierungen im Text und Notizen darauf vorbereiten, ihrem Partner anschließend die Grafik(en) zu beschreiben und erklären. Unbekannter Wortschatz, der für das Textverständnis unabdingbar ist, kann in (online) Wörterbüchern nachgeschlagen werden. Es wurde bewusst auf Verständnisfragen verzichtet, um ein bloßes Diktieren oder gegenseitiges Abschreiben der Ergebnisse in der Partnerarbeit zu verhindern. Die Versprachlichung und Erläuterung der Grafiken führt zu einem authentischen, komplexen Sprechanlass.

authentischer Sprachaustausch

Vertieft wird diese reproduktive Phase durch die Frage, wie beide Texte inhaltlich in Bezug zueinander zu bringen sind. In einem abschließenden Unterrichtsgespräch werden eventuelle Fragen geklärt und der inhaltliche Bezug der Texte besprochen.

Detroit – a two-sided city (KV 8)

Ein Text über Detroit, Schauplatz des Filmes, bietet zusätzliches Hintergrundwissen zur Entwicklung der Stadt von der Nachkriegszeit bis zur Gegenwart. Zwar liegt der Fokus des Artikels auf der aktuellen Situation der Metropole, doch er erklärt auch, warum Walts Nachbarschaft einen radikalen demografischen Wandel vollzogen hat. Der Text kann auch sehr gut erst zu einem beliebigen späteren Zeitpunkt bearbeitet werden, da sich dann der Bezug zum Film herstellen lässt.

flexibler Einsatz des Textes

Lernziel: SuS können Multiple Choice Fragen zu einem Artikel über Detroit lösen und ihre Antworten durch Zitate korrekt belegen. Falls die SuS den Film bereits gesehen haben, können sie Informationen aus dem Text mit dem Schauplatz des Films Gran Torino in Verbindung setzen.
Material: Text (KV 8)
Sozialform: Einzelarbeit, Partnerarbeit, Unterrichtsgespräch
Ablauf: Als Pre-reading Aufgabe können die SuS aufgefordert werden, in Partnerarbeit oder im Plenum ihr Vorwissen über Detroit zusammenzutragen. Anschließend bearbeiten sie die Leseverständnisfragen zum Text individuell. Die Ergebnissicherung erfolgt lehrerzentriert im Plenum. Es bietet sich an zur Eingangsfrage zurückzukehren und die SuS ihr Vorwissen mit den Informationen aus dem Artikel abgleichen zu lassen. Eine weiterführende Fragestellung könnte lauten: *Point out the relevance of the information that the article provides for the understanding of the movie.* Diese kann auch als Zusatzaufgabe für SuS genutzt werden, welche die Multiple Choice Aufgabe besonders schnell lösen.

Speed dating: Films and me

What role do films play in your life?

What movies have you recently watched? Would you recommend them?

What is your all-time favorite movie?

What film genres (drama/comedy/action/science fiction/romance/western…) do you like to watch?

Name the main reasons why you watch a film (entertainment, distraction, information, seeing other worlds)?

Where and how do you watch movies most often: at the movie theater/at home on TV/anywhere on your smartphone/tablet…?

What do you prefer: films from the US, Germany, France, India, Africa, …?

Do you know movies by Clint Eastwood? How do you like him as a director and/or actor?

If you were an actor, what role would suit you best?

If you were given the chance to direct a film, what kind of film would it be? What setting would you choose? Which actors would you ask?

Film terminology: How to analyse a film

Here are some illustrations of the most important film terminology for use in your discussions.

Camera movements *(Bildausschnitt / Bildgröße)*

static shot: camera does not move

to zoom in on / out of sth. (e.g. a face)

to pan left / right *horizontal schwenken*; to tilt up / down *vertikal schwenken*

tracking shot *(Kamerafahrt)*: camera is on a vehicle moving on the ground

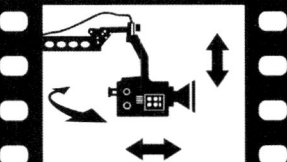

crane shot *(Kranfahrt)*: camera moves flexibly in all directions on a crane

hand-held camera

Field size
(Bildausschnitt / Bildgröße)

long shot *(Totale)*; people / objects shown from a distance

full shot: shot of the whole body / object

medium shot: upper body / part of an object

close-up *(Nahaufnahme)*: head and shoulders

extreme close-up: *(Detailaufnahme)* face only; detailed shot

Camera angles

high-angle shot (from above)

eyelevel shot

low-angle shot (from below)

Camera positions

A point-of-view shot is seen through a character's eyes. Other examples are:

establishing shot: shows location (long shot / pan at the start of a scene)

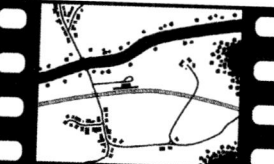

Top shot or God's eye view

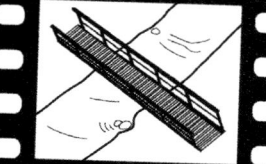

overhead shot: bird's eye view

over-the-shoulder shot

reverse-angle shot: from the opposite side, usu. shows a dialogue partner

Gran Torino: Movie trailer

1. *Read through the adjectives in the box and make sure that you understand what they mean. They are all taken from film reviews of Gran Torino. Copy them into the table, sorting them into positive, neutral and negative adjectives. Add more adjectives which can be used to describe and evaluate a film and sort them.*

> realistic – vigorous (forceful, dynamic) – predictable – touching – humorous – insightful – macho –
> gritty (unsentimental, harsh) – clichéd – entertaining – well-paced (with a good speed) –
> earnest (serious, intense) – thought-provoking – radical – compelling (convincing, fascinating)

Positive	Neutral	Negative

2. *Watch the trailer and choose three to five adjectives that you consider to be most OR least suitable to describe the movie, judging from the trailer. Discuss your choice with your partner.*

3. *The trailer reveals conflicts between different characters or groups of characters. Watch the trailer again and use arrows to indicate where you think conflicts exist in the character web. Highlight the conflicts you expect to be most dominant in the movie.*

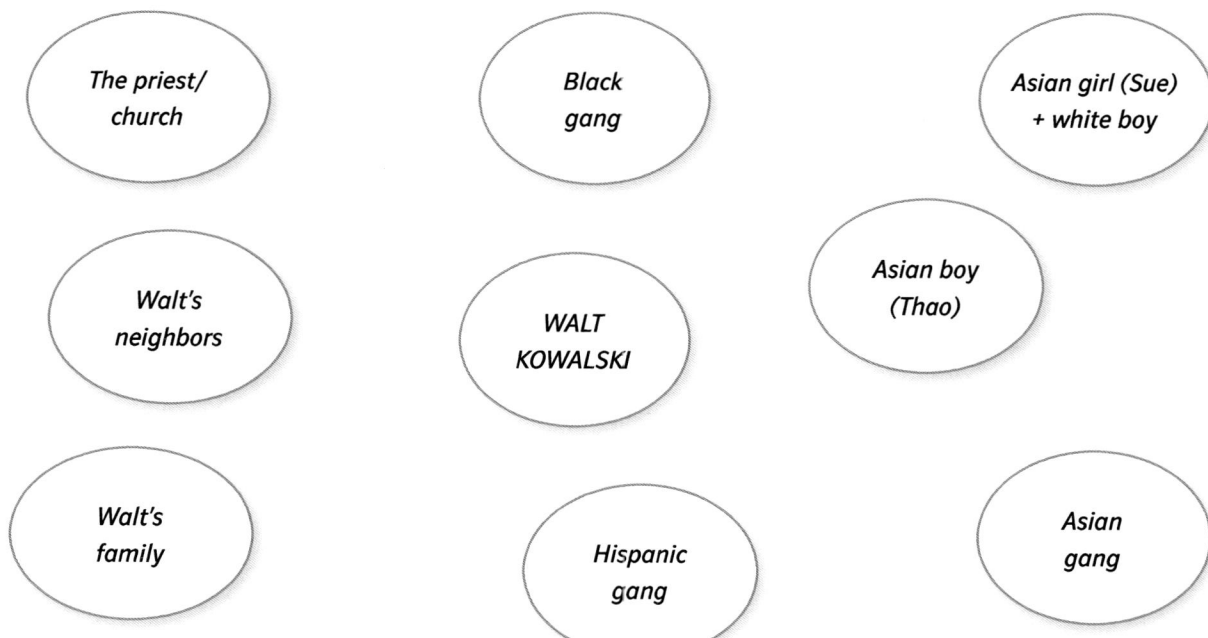

Gran Torino: Movie poster

1. *Look closely at the poster and make a rough sketch of the picture in the box below. Focus on lines, shapes and contrasts. Interpret your findings and discuss them with your neighbor. The expressions below might help.*

a horizontal / vertical / straight / diagonal line
There is a clear / well-defined / straight line that runs from … to …
The most dominant lines in the foreground …
The shape of the lines reminds me of … / resembles …
There is a(n) obvious / remarkable / sharp contrast between … and …
X and Y form / express a stark / striking / strong contrast, which could stand for …
The contrast might mirror … / could be interpreted as …

2. *Write down anything you associate with the movie poster right into your sketch.*

3. *With your partner, speculate about the movie's possible genre, storyline (plot) and themes.*

Gran Torino: Speed viewing

1. *Universal themes are general ideas about the human condition. They deal with human concerns that are not influenced or caused by cultural differences or where we live. They raise questions about the relationship of human beings to themselves, to each other and to the universe. Make sure you know the meaning of all the themes in the list. Mark the ones that personally concern you now. Share your thoughts about one or two of them with your neighbour if you feel comfortable with this.*

abundance/scarcity	*freedom*	*peer pressure*
abuse of power	*friendship*	*perseverance*
action vs. apathy	*greed*	*prejudice*
authority	*guilt and innocence*	*pride*
beauty	*heritage*	*quest for knowledge*
coming of age	*heroes*	*religion*
courage	*honesty*	*repentance*
effects of the past	*justice*	*revenge*
faith	*love and hate*	*security/safety*
family	*loyalty*	*seizing the moment*
fate	*need for change*	*survival*
fear	*obligation*	*the road not taken*
fear of failure	*parent-child relationships*	*war and peace*

2. *Watch the first half of the movie in the 16X fast forward mode. From the list of universal themes choose at least five you think play a major role in the movie. Justify and discuss your choice with your neighbor.*

3. *Even though Clint Eastwood's movie deals with universal themes, it is clearly a product of its culture. Watch the first half of the movie again – this time in the 16X rewind mode – and note down moments or images you consider to be typically American. Explain what ideas you connect with these "American moments" or icons and what they stand for. Discuss if they relate to any of the universal themes in particular.*

American moment/icon   ➜   **What it stands for...**

4. *The speed viewing doesn't really help us understand the title of the movie. Think of an alternative title that captures themes and symbols you see as central to the film. Discuss your ideas with your neighbor.*

© Ernst Klett Sprachen GmbH, Stuttgart 2017 | www.klett-sprachen.de | Alle Rechte vorbehalten.
Kopieren für den eigenen Unterrichtsgebrauch gestattet.
ISBN 978-3-12-577484-1

Historical background

1. *Read the text and be prepared to explain the context of the photo and the map below to your partner (highlight relevant passages, take notes).*

2. *Once you have exchanged your information find connections between the two texts.*

The Korean War (1950–1953)

US Corsair fighter planes over a US warship during the Korean War. Sept 4 1951.

5

10

15

World War II divided Korea into a Communist northern half and an American-occupied southern half, divided at the 38th parallel. The Korean War (1950–1953) began when the North Korean Communist army crossed the 38th Parallel and invaded non-Communist South Korea. As the North Korean army, armed with Soviet tanks, quickly overran South Korea, the United States came to South Korea's aid. General Douglas MacArthur, who had been overseeing the post-WWII occupation of Japan, commanded the US forces, which now began to hold off the North Koreans at Busan, at the southernmost tip of Korea. Although Korea was not strategically essential to the United States, the political environment of the Cold War at this stage was such that policymakers did not want to appear "soft on Communism." Officially, the US intervened as part of a "police action" run by a UN (United Nations) international peace-keeping force; in actuality, the UN was simply being manipulated by US and NATO anti-Communist interests.

20

In 1953, an armistice agreement was signed at Panmunjom that effectively – if not actually technically ended the Korean War, returning Korea to a divided status which was essentially the same as before the war. Furthermore, neither the war nor its outcome did much to lessen the era's Cold War tension.

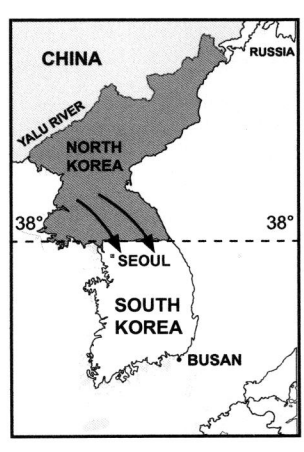

June 25, 1950

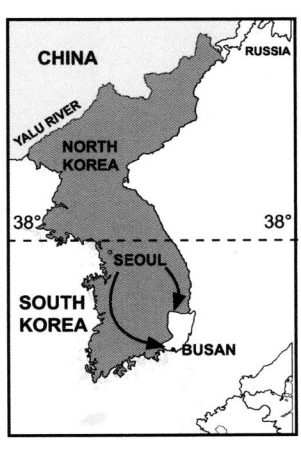

Sept. 14, 1950

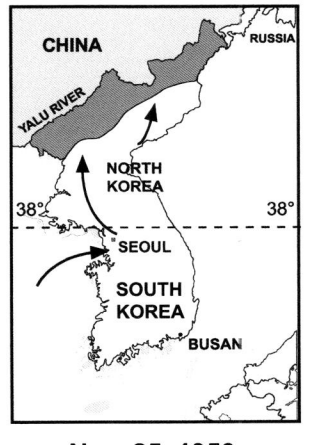

Nov. 25, 1950

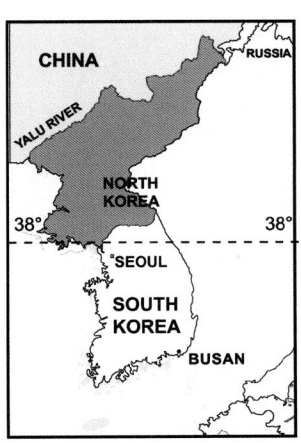

July 27, 1953

Historical background

1. *Read the text and be prepared to explain the link between the photo and the map below to your partner (highlight relevant passages, take notes).*
2. *Once you have exchanged your information find connections between the two texts.*

The Hmong and the "Secret War" (1964–1973)

Vietnam Veteran's Memorial in Washington DC.

The Secret War began around the time the US became officially involved in the Vietnam War. In the early 1960s, the US Central Intelligence Agency (CIA) began to recruit, train and lead the indigenous Hmong people in Laos to join fighting the Vietnam War.
5 The Hmong ([mãŋ]), are an Asian ethnic group from the mountainous regions of China, Vietnam, Laos, and Thailand. About 60 % of all Hmong men in Laos joined the "Secret War". Hmong soldiers put their lives at risk in the front line, fighting for the US to block the supply line and to rescue downed American pilots. From 1967–1971, 3,772 Hmong
10 soldiers were killed in the war, 5,426 injured or disabled.

Following the US withdrawal from Vietnam in 1975, the Lao kingdom was overthrown by the communists and the Hmong people became targets of retaliation and persecution. While some Hmong people returned to their villages and attempted to resume life under the new regime, thousands more fled to Thailand, often under attack. This marked the beginning of a mass exodus of Hmong people from Laos. Those who did make it
15 to Thailand generally were held in squalid United Nations refugee camps.

Many Hmong refugees were resettled in the United States after the Vietnam War. Beginning in December 1975, the first of them arrived in the U.S., mainly from refugee camps in Thailand; however, only 3,466 were granted asylum. In May 1976, another 11,000 were allowed to enter the United States, and by 1978 some 30,000 Hmong people had immigrated. It was not until the passage of the Refugee Act of 1980 that families were
20 able to enter the US, becoming the second wave of Hmong immigrants. Today, about 210,000 Hmong people reside in the United States. The majority of these live in three federal states: California (ca 66,000), Minnesota (46,000) and Wisconsin (32,000).

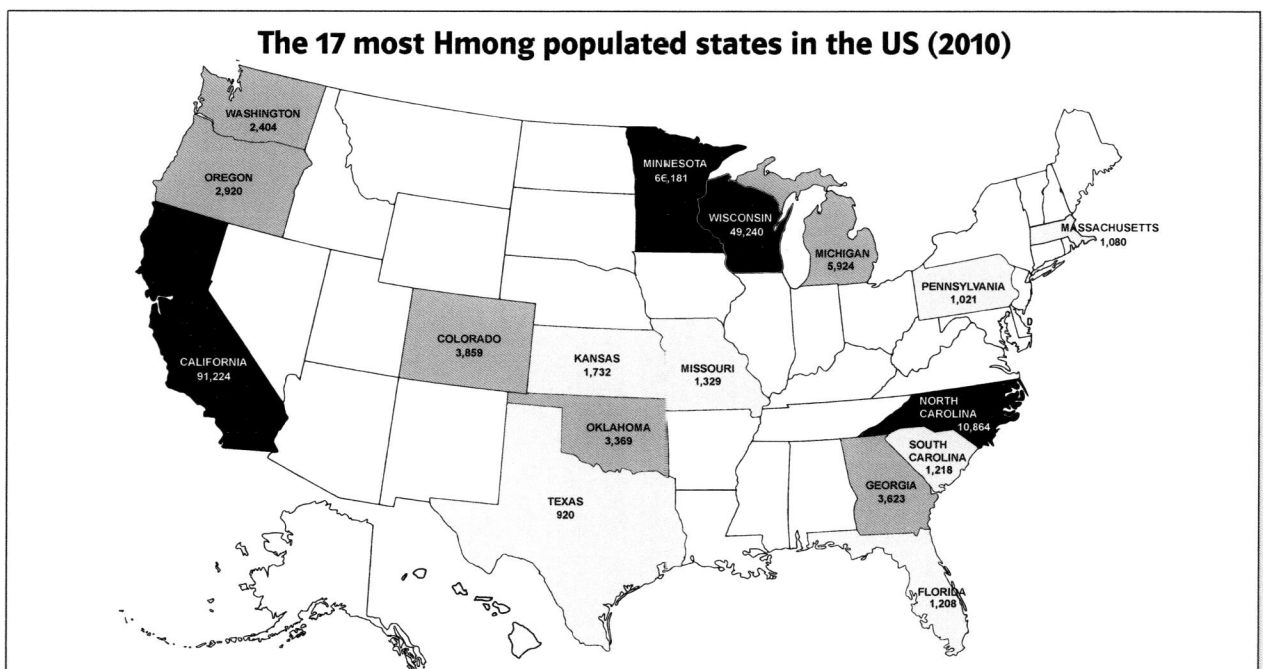

The 17 most Hmong populated states in the US (2010)

WASHINGTON 2,404
OREGON 2,920
MINNESOTA 66,181
WISCONSIN 49,240
MICHIGAN 5,924
MASSACHUSETTS 1,080
PENNSYLVANIA 1,021
CALIFORNIA 91,224
COLORADO 3,859
KANSAS 1,732
MISSOURI 1,329
NORTH CAROLINA 10,864
SOUTH CAROLINA 1,218
OKLAHOMA 3,369
GEORGIA 3,623
TEXAS 920
FLORIDA 1,208

8 **supply line** – *Versorgungszufuhr*; 12 **retaliation** – revenge; 15 **squalid** – dirty, neglected

Detroit – the two-sided city

In 1903 Henry Ford founded the Ford Motor Company in Detroit, establishing the city's status as the world's automotive capital – "Motor City". With the expansion of the automobile industry in the early 20th century, Detroit became the fourth largest city in the country. Industrial restructuring and loss of jobs in the auto industry led to a considerable loss in population from the late 20th century to the present
5 *– from a peak population of 1.8 million in 1950 to less than 714,000 in 2011. In 2013, the city of Detroit declared a financial emergency and filed for bankruptcy, which was successfully exited in 2014.*

For the past two years, I have taken postgraduate students in urban geography to Detroit, where
10 a prosperous downtown is rising. The city's transformation is being celebrated and seen as a potential model for other places.

But George Galster, professor of urban studies at Detroit's Wayne State University told my
15 students to imagine the city as a bathtub. The new investments and activities are like water pouring into the tub. But nothing has been done to plug the giant hole at the bottom of the tub. This new renaissance does not address why Detroit
20 declined in the first place. It does little to address poverty, unemployment and access to resources

Detroit, 2015. The Renaissance Center in downtown (left).

for the vast majority of the city's residents. What's worse, the <u>gentrification</u> of downtown Detroit contributes to greater inequality and polarisation, which are growing challenges for cities around the world. What has created this hole at the bottom of the bathtub?
25 Between 2000 and 2010, 25 % of the population left the city – that's an average of 2,000 people a month. Half of its 5–9 year olds departed during this time, their parents leaving in search of better schools and opportunities in the suburbs. Today, Motor City boasts just two vehicle assembly plants, down from more than two dozen at its peak. Neighbourhoods which used to house factory workers look like rural prairie. This exodus of jobs has led to a mismatch of people and employment across
30 the region. Around 60 % of Detroiters who have a job work in the suburbs. Conversely, 70 % of the jobs located in the city of Detroit go to people who live in the suburbs. Chronic unemployment and poverty remain one of the city's biggest challenges.

The current renaissance does not address these problems. Most investment takes place in the Greater Downtown, which includes the city's historic core and neighbourhoods such as Midtown and
35 Corktown, which comprise 5 % of the city's area and population. Here, once-abandoned offices are being bought up and renovated by enthusiastic entrepreneurs, a new modern tram line is being built along Woodward Avenue and it can actually be difficult to find an apartment as vacancy rates are very low. The boundaries between revival and decay can be very severe. Travel three minutes by car from Midtown's Wayne State University and you are surrounded by streets overgrown by vegetation and
40 burned out factories.

Greater Downtown's current revival will mean that this 5 % of the city will pull further and further ahead of the other 95 %. Those able to afford to live there enjoy great restaurants and bars, well-paid employment, safe and attractive neighbourhoods and reliable public transit. The problem is most Detroiters cannot afford to live here. And like everything else in Southeast Michigan, race is one of the

22 **gentrification** when middle-class people move into (and take over) neighbourhoods where poor people live

45 dominant factors. In a city that is 85 % African American, Greater Downtown is becoming increasingly white.

There are also growing divides between public and private services. While most Detroiters wait hours for the police to arrive, private security forces patrol Downtown and around Wayne State University. When problems arise in adjacent neighbourhoods, you don't call 911, you call campus
50 police, who respond in minutes, rather than hours. New public transport investments are increasingly focusing on Detroit's core. There is a sad irony that in a city where about a quarter of residents are too poor to own a car, the new tram line will serve office workers and students in Greater Downtown. It will do nothing for the low-income families that need to travel 15 km by bus to access a basic grocery store. So while there is indeed a "renaissance" taking place in Detroit, most city residents are detached
55 from it.

This inequality is part and parcel of contemporary cities. It is not confined to cities struggling with the legacy of de-industrialisation; polarisation is also one of the biggest challenges facing prosperous cities such as London, New York or Paris. But inequality doesn't just happen. It is the product of economic, business and political decisions of what, how and where to invest and distribute money
60 and resources.

Brian Doucet, in *The Guardian*, 17 February 2015

Read the text and tick the correct statement as indicated. Use a quotation from the text to support your decision. Give the line number(s) plus the first three and the last three words of the quotation. If the quotation is less than six words, write down the full quotation. EXTRA: Speculate on connections between the text and the movie.

1. The bathtub metaphor tries to illustrate

   ☐ that downtown Detroit has become a prosperous, comfortable place.
   ☐ that the development of the city serves as a model for other cities.
   ☐ that recent investments have little effect on the poor.
   ☐ that recent investments have finally plugged up the hole in the bathtub.

   Line(s) … ✐ _____

2. In the past 15 years Detroit has changed because

   ☐ many car plants were moved to the suburbs.
   ☐ many families fled to the suburbs.
   ☐ neighbourhoods where workers used to live have become gentrified.
   ☐ most jobs are located in the Greater Downtown.

   Line(s) … ✐ _____

3. Midtown and Corktown are neighbourhoods

   ☐ where you can only live if you have a decent income.
   ☐ that haven't profited from the recent revival.
   ☐ where whites are a minority.
   ☐ where you depend on a car.

   Line(s) … ✐ _____

Klett

II   Filmarbeit: Modul A: Theme Club Project (KV A1 – A8)

Konzept

Ziel dieses lernerorientierten Unterrichtsmoduls ist es, die SuS zu einer weitgehend selbständigen Auseinandersetzung mit dem Film anzuleiten. In Projektgruppen beschäftigen sie sich intensiv mit einem von fünf zentralen Themen des Films: *Prejudices and Racism*, *Masculinity*, *Gran Torino*, *Violence* und *Religion*. Dabei erweitern sie ihren Wortschatz durch nützliche Chunks und schulen ihre Filmkompetenz, indem sie Motive und Themen des Films analysieren und den Film als ästhetisches Kunstwerk verstehen lernen. Ein besonderes Anliegen des Konzept ist es, die SuS persönlich zu involvieren und im geschützten Raum der Kleingruppe zum Sprachhandeln zu motivieren, d.h. zum Austauschen von Informationen und Meinungen, zum Diskutieren und Sich-Einigen.

behandelte Themen

Individuell auf jede Gruppe zugeschnittene Aufgabenblätter liefern das nötige Scaffolding, um den sprachlichen und inhaltlichen Lernzuwachs zu gewährleisten. So gibt es für jede Themengruppe ein einseitiges *Language Sheet*, das entweder nur die SuS der entsprechenden Themengruppe oder aber alle individuell bearbeiten. Die Lösungshinweise zu allen *Language Sheets* finden sich zur Selbstkorrektur im Schülerbuch. Für die inhaltliche und kinematografische Auseinandersetzung mit dem Film stehen themenspezifische Task Sheets zur Verfügung. Die Task Sheets aller Themengruppen sind gleich aufgebaut:

themenbasierte Language Sheets (KV A1.L bis A5.L, S. 42–46)

entsprechende themenbasierte Task Sheets

Task 1: *Getting started* (pre-viewing activity): Heranführung an das Thema.
Task 2: *Watching the movie* (while-viewing): Beobachtungsauftrag für den gesamten Film.
Task 3: *Watching closely* (while-viewing/reading/listening): Inhaltliche und filmästhetische Analyse einer ausgewählten Filmszene.
Task 4: *Exploring further* (post-viewing): Diskussionsfrage zum Film oder über den Film hinaus.

Das klar strukturierte Aufgabenarrangement der Task Sheets bereitet die SuS inhaltlich, sprachlich und methodisch darauf vor, sich eigenverantwortlich und in Abstimmung mit der Gruppe eine geeignete Filmszene für eine abschließende Präsentation auszuwählen und diese zu analysieren und zu interpretieren. Diese mündliche Präsentation kann durch eine schriftliche Fixierung zentraler Arbeitsergebnisse der Gruppe auf einem Poster oder in Form einer digitalen Kurzpräsentation (z. B. ein Slide pro SuS) unterstützt werden.

Organisation und Ablauf

Die fünf Themen können auf verschiedene Gruppen verteilt werden.
Als Lehrkraft können Sie aber auch nur zwei oder drei Themen auswählen und diese jeweils von mehreren Gruppen bearbeiten lassen. Im Idealfall wählen die SuS ihr Thema selbst, dabei sollte das leicht unterschiedliche Anspruchsniveau der Aufgabenstellungen transparent gemacht werden (siehe: **Kommentare zu den Themengruppen** auf Seite 28–29). Es kann auch sinnvoll sein, dafür zu sorgen, dass in jeder Gruppe mindestens ein leistungsstärkerer Schüler oder eine leistungsstärkere Schülerin mitarbeitet, damit die Qualität der Arbeitsergebnisse der einzelnen Gruppen nicht zu sehr divergiert.

Wahl und Einsatz der Themen

Gruppenbildung

Nachdem die Lehrkraft den SuS das Konzept erläutert hat, werden noch vor der Sichtung des Films die Themengruppen gebildet, die entsprechenden Aufgabenblätter ausgeteilt und Task 1 bearbeitet. Es handelt sich hierbei um eine Speaking Activity, die zur persönlichen Involvierung jedes Einzelnen in das Thema beiträgt und durch die kommunikative Aufgabenstellung den Gruppenbildungsprozess unterstützt.

Im Anschluss machen sich die SuS mit der Aufgabenstellung der Task 2 vertraut. Diese umfasst eine themenspezifische Beobachtungsaufgabe für den ganzen Film, die während der Sichtung schriftlich bearbeitet und nachträglich ergänzt werden kann.

Film spielen lassen

Der 112-minütige Film wird zentral ohne gewollte Unterbrechung gezeigt, wozu etwa 2½ Schulstunden benötigt werden. Die schulstundenbedingte Unterbrechung kann genutzt werden, um Spekulationen zum weiteren Handlungsverlauf anzustellen.

SuS-Reaktionen auf den Film: drei Möglichkeiten

Nach Abschluss der Filmsichtung sollten die SuS die Möglichkeit bekommen, persönliche Eindrücke, Reaktionen und Meinungen zum Film zum Ausdruck zu bringen. Dies kann in der Themengruppe, im Partnergespräch oder im Plenum erfolgen. Als möglicher Impuls kann eine Bewertung mit Sternen dienen. Die SuS entscheiden, mit wie vielen Sternen sie den Film bewerten würden:

Möglichkeit 1: Bewertung mit Sternen

Ein Stern, falls ihnen der Film nicht zusagt und sie ihn nicht weiterempfehlen würden, fünf Sterne, falls der Film zu einen der besten zählt, den sie je gesehen haben und sie ihn unbedingt weiterempfehlen würden. Die Bewertung muss dabei begründet werden.

Möglichkeit 2: Pre-Viewing Activity, siehe Seite 13

Alternativ kann die Adjektivliste der Pre-viewing Activity zum Trailer (KV 3, S. 18) genutzt werden, die SuS dazu aufzufordern, sich persönlich zum Film zu äußern.

Möglichkeit 3: Skizzen

Eine dritte methodische Option ist, die SuS individuell eine Skizze von einer Szene anfertigen zu lassen, die sie besonders beeindruckt oder berührt hat.
Die Ergebnisse werden mit einem oder mehreren Partnern ausgetauscht.
Die anderen stellen zunächst Vermutungen an um welche Szene es sich handelt.
Außerdem kommentiert jede(r) SuS warum er oder sie diese Szene gewählt hat.

Ergebnisse und Diskussion

Nachdem alle SuS die individuelle Bearbeitung der Task 2 abgeschlossen haben, werden die Ergebnisse in der Gruppe verglichen und durch eine Diskussion vertieft.

Task 3: Watching closely

Zur Bearbeitung der themenspezifischen *Watching closely* Task 3 ist ein wiederholtes Ansehen einer einzelnen Filmszene erforderlich. Die Filmszenen sind (Stand Januar 2016) auf YouTube verfügbar und können entweder im Unterricht oder aber zuhause individuell mit Tablets oder Smartphones und Kopfhörern gesichtet werden. Die Diskussionsfrage der letzten Task *(Exploring further)* stellt einen offenen Sprechanlass dar, der das Thema oder den Film in einen größeren Kontext setzt.
Haben die Gruppen ihre Aufgabenstellungen der Task Sheets abgeschlossen, bereiten sie ihre Präsentation vor.

Transfer: Präsentation

Dazu wählt jede Gruppe eine Filmszene aus und präsentiert anhand dieser eine Zusammenfassung und ggf. einen Transfer der Arbeitsergebnisse. Poster oder digitale Präsentationen können zur Fixierung oder Visualisierung genutzt werden. Dies kann von der Lehrkraft festgelegt oder den SuS freigestellt werden. Nach der

Phase des vorbereiteten monologischen Sprechens der Präsentation sollten sich die SuS in einer kurzen Frage- oder Diskussionsrunde auch spontan und frei zu bestimmten Aspekten ihres Themas äußern können. Hierfür können die zuhörenden SuS bereits vor der Präsentation den Auftrag bekommen, eine oder zwei Fragen an die Gruppe oder einzelne Gruppenmitglieder zu notieren. Die Lehrkraft kann ergänzend Sprechimpulse vor allem für zurückhaltende SuS geben.

Die individuellen Beiträge der Gruppenpräsentation können zur punktuellen mündlichen Leistungsmessung herangezogen werden. Dabei wird sowohl das etwa dreiminütige vorbereitete monologische Sprechen als auch das spontane Sprechen in der anschließenden Fragerunde bewertet.

Leistungsmessung

Um die Ergebnisse aller Themengruppen zusammenzuführen steht ein Arbeitsblatt (KV A8) mit einem *Theme Web* zur Verfügung, auf welchem sich Zusammenhänge zwischen den einzelnen Themen visualisieren und notieren lassen. Als alle Themen umfassende und vertiefende Aufgabe dient die Analyse der kulturbedingten Wertvorstellungen, die sich in den einzelnen Themen widerspiegeln und die das nationale Selbstverständnis der Amerikaner ausmachen. Abschließend bietet sich ein Vergleich mit dem nationalen Selbstverständnis der Deutschen an.

Zusammenhänge zwischen den Themen über Theme Web

Möglicher Zeit- und Materialplan

0. (einführende) Stunde	Hinführung zum Thema Film (KV 1) Einführung in die Filmanalyse (KV 2)
1. Stunde	• Pre-viewing Activity im Plenum (KV 3, KV 4 oder KV 5) • Historical Background (KV 6 und KV 7) • Organisation der Theme Groups (KV A1 – A5) • Task 1: *Getting started* in der Themengruppe Alternative: Hintergrundrecherche "The Hmong and the „Secret War"/„Korean War" als vorbereitende HA
2. – 4. Stunde	• Filmsichtung *straight-through* (112 min) • Task 2: *Watching the movie* • Abschließend persönliche Reaktionen/Eindrücke/ Meinungen der SuS abfragen • Hausaufgabe: Language Sheet (KV A1.L – A5.L); • Task 3: *Watching closely* (wenn Filmszenen nicht individuell im Unterricht noch einmal auf YouTube angeschaut werden können)
5. + 6. Stunde	• Bearbeitung und/oder Auswertung von Task 3 in der Gruppe. • Bearbeitung Task 4: *Exploring further* in der Gruppe. Hausaufgabe: Landeskundlicher Text über Detroit als Leseverstehensübung (KV 8)
7. Stunde	Vorbereitung der Präsentation (KV A6)
8. + 9. Stunde	Präsentationen mit kurzer Fragerunde, Zusammenführung der Ergebnisse (KV A7 & A8)

Kommentare zu den Themengruppen

Prejudice and racism

Lernziele	Die SuS können ihre Meinungen und Erfahrungen zum Thema Rassismus im Alltag zum Ausdruck bringen. Sie können Walts rassistische Äußerungen und Verhaltensweisen im Film beschreiben und Walts Entwicklung visualisieren. Sie können Walts Vorurteile gegenüber den Hmong in einer Filmszene wiedergeben und Sues Reaktionen darauf beschreiben. Sie können aufzeigen wie Sue durch die kinematografische Darstellungsweise auf Augenhöhe mit Walt erscheint. Sie können über mögliche Ursachen für Walts Rassismus sprechen. Unterstützt durch einen Artikel können die SuS diskutieren, ob Gran Torino ein Film über Rassismus oder auch ein rassistischer Film ist.
Material	KV A1 und KV A1.L (Seiten 30 bzw. 42)
Anspruch	Die Aufgabenstellungen dieser Themengruppe entsprechen inhaltlich und sprachlich **einem durchschnittlichen Anspruchsniveau**. Quantitativ sind es die umfangreichsten Task Sheets, die sich für zügig arbeitende SuS anbieten.

Masculinity

Lernziel	Die SuS werden sich stereotypischer Beschreibungen von Männlichkeit und Weiblichkeit in ihrer eigenen Kultur und der Zielkultur bewusst und können diese kritisch hinterfragen. Sie können die Inszenierung von Walts und Thaos (mangelnder) Männlichkeit im Film beschreiben, analysieren und kritisch reflektieren. Die SuS können sich äußern, welche Frauenrolle Sue in diesem von Männern dominierten Film spielt.
Material	KV A2, ggf. Zusatzmaterial: Dokumentationen auf der Spielfilm-DVD Gran Torino („Die Bemannung des Rades") und KV A2.L (Seiten 33 bzw. 43)
Anspruch	Die Aufgabenstellungen dieser Themengruppe entsprechen inhaltlich und sprachlich **einem durchschnittlichen Anspruchsniveau**. Da sie leicht zugänglich sind und kein besonders großes Abstraktion- oder Assoziationsvermögen erfordern, können sie auch von leistungsschwächeren SuS gut bewältigt werden.

Gran Torino

Lernziel	Ausgehend von Zitaten über die (stereotypische) Bedeutung von Autos für Männer, können die SuS ihre eigenen Meinungen und Erfahrungen zum Ausdruck bringen. Sie können Filmszenen, in denen der Gran Torino eine Rolle spielt, beschreiben und die Bedeutung dieses Wagens für Walt und Thao und deren Freundschaft interpretieren. Durch die Analyse von zwei kurzen Filmszenen können die SuS erkennen wie Gefühle der Protagonisten kinematografisch kommuniziert werden. Die SuS können den Film in Bezug setzen zu anderen Filmen, in denen Autos unterschiedliche Rollen spielen.
Material	KV A3, ggf. Zusatzmaterial: Dokumentationen auf der Spielfilm-DVD Gran Torino („Gran Torino: Mehr als nur ein Auto") und KV A3.L (Seiten 35 bzw. 44)
Anspruch	Die Aufgabenstellungen dieser Themengruppe entsprechen inhaltlich und sprachlich **einem durchschnittlichen Anspruchsniveau**. Da sie bis auf eine Extra-Aufgabe leicht zugänglich sind und kein besonders großes Abstraktion- oder Assoziationsvermögen erfordern, können sie auch von leistungsschwächeren SuS gut bewältigt werden.

Violence

Lernziel	Die SuS können die Eskalation eines Konflikts beschreiben und mit ihren eigenen Erfahrungen in Bezug setzen. Sie können Schlüsselszenen der Gewalteskalation im Spielfilm beschreiben und diese unterschiedlichen Gewaltstufen zuordnen. Sie können über Möglichkeiten der Deeskalation diskutieren. Die SuS können sich zur Bedeutung einer der bekanntesten Szenen des Films („Get off my lawn") äußern und analysieren, welche atmosphärische Wirkung Filmtechniken haben und wie sie Spannung erzeugen. Die SuS können den Film als kulturellen Spiegel der amerikanischen Gesellschaft deuten.
Material	KV A4 und KV A4.L (Seiten 38 bzw. 45)
Anspruch	Die Aufgabenstellungen dieser Themengruppe entsprechen inhaltlich und sprachlich **einem durchschnittlichen Anspruchsniveau.**

Religion

Lernziel	Die SuS können christliche Symbole und ihre Bedeutung beschreiben und christliche Motive in Gran Torino erkennen und Deutungsversuche diskutieren. Sie können die kinematografische Darstellungsweise der Todesszene analysieren und interpretieren. Die SuS können Walts Form der Buße mit der des katholischen Glaubens vergleichen und sich persönlich dazu äußern. Sie können über die These, dass Medien die Rolle einer unsichtbaren Religion in unsere Kultur spielen, diskutieren.
Material	KV A5 und KV A5.L (Seiten 40 bzw. 46)
Anspruch	Die Aufgabenstellungen dieser Themengruppe sind inhaltlich und sprachlich **sehr anspruchsvoll und eignen sich besonders für leistungsstärkere SuS**. Sie erfordern ein großes Abstraktions- und Assoziationsvermögen und einen themenspezifischen Wortschatz, mit dem die SuS nicht unbedingt vorab vertraut sind.

Task sheets for theme group: Prejudice and racism

1. Getting started: Everyday racism

What language do you speak in Korea? Asian?

a. *Discuss what this real life situation reveals about the speaker's mindset. Share examples of everyday racism that you have experienced or witnessed and discuss what options you have to react to overtly racist remarks or jokes.*

"The less secure a man is, the more likely he is to have extreme prejudice."
"People have lost their sense of humor. In former times, we constantly made jokes about different races."

b. *In your group discuss the meaning and validity of Clint Eastwood's above remarks on racism.*

2. Watching the movie: Walt Kowalski's racism

a. *Racism is about more than words. Take notes to describe how Walt Kowalski expresses his racism.*

LANGUAGE *What he says and how he says it:*	BEHAVIOR/ACTIONS *How he behaves towards the Hmong:*

b. *Examine if Walt's racism undergoes a development in the course of the movie. Visualize your findings graphically or in a drawing. Compare your findings in your group and agree on one visualization.*

c. *Discuss if Walt is a through and through racist, a racist at heart, or if his racism is only a manly façade.*

3. Watching closely: Roots of racism

a. *After rescuing Sue from the black gang. Walt talks to her for the first time in his truck. Closely watch chapter 10 again (DVD 00:34:48 – 00:38:33/YouTube: Gran Torino (clip 6 – part 2) "Where the hell is Humong, I mean Hmong, anyway?"). Analyze what Walt thinks about the Hmong and how Sue reacts.*

Walt's preconception about the Hmong	Sue's reactions

b. *"Racism is rooted in ignorance". Discuss this statement in reference to the scene. Find other reasons for Walt's racism.*

c. *At the beginning of the scene, Sue is the victim who is rescued by Walt. In the course of the conversation, however, Sue proves that she can easily keep up with Walt. Analyze the cinematic techniques that are used to emphasize that Walt and Sue are on the same level.*

Camera angle	Field size

➜ Although Walt is clearly taller and physically stronger than Sue, the way the camera presents them emphasizes that…

4. Exploring further: Eastwood accused of racism

a. *Gran Torino has definitely raised people's awareness for the history and culture of the Hmong minority in the US, but there are also many critical voices. Read the text, highlight the accusations against Eastwood and come up with counter-arguments.*

> Though many of the people who have seen the film may have gotten a sense of satisfaction and joy from seeing that Walt overcame his racism, the people who acted as the Hmong members in the movie did not. They were offended by the traces of racism that were included in the movie and that they experienced themselves on set.
>
> 5   Vang, who played Thao in the film, said he and the other Hmong actors were treated unfairly. Eastwood would not allow them to tweak their lines (even though he claimed that he did allow them to when asked in interviews following the release of the movie) […].
>
> The actors felt degraded when they were told to "make noise" by rambling words in their language. The Hmong actors were also left out by their fellow cast members who were white.
>
> 10   The cast members excluded them from cast events because they immediately assumed that Hmong actors were exactly like their character counterparts—unable to speak English clearly or to understand anything "American."
>
> Vang also mentioned that he was upset by the way the Hmongs were portrayed in the film. He did not want the Hmong community—his own community—to be seen in a negative light by the
>
> 15   audience. He pointed out that tea ceremonies were not performed correctly, that some of their important political lines in the script were not subtitled into English, and that these inaccuracies led to misconceptions of the community. […]
>
> The movie itself contained many racial slurs about Asians that the speakers found insulting.
>
> In the scene in which Walt takes Thao to his friend's barber shop, Thao is called names such as
>
> 20   "pussy kid," "dick smoking Guk head" and "chink." These degrading words imply that Asians are feminine and homosexual.
>
> From: thebottomline.as.ucsb.edu

b. *In your group act out a round table with Clint Eastwood, Nick Schenk (spreenplay writer), Bee Vang (Thao Van Lor) and Ahney Her (Sue Lor). Take roles. Discuss whether Gran Torino is a movie about racism or a racist movie.*

Notes

Task sheets for theme group: Masculinity

1. Getting started: The man card

A "man card" doesn't really exist. It is an imaginary "certificate" which shows that a man is a "respectable" member of the male community and has proven that he is "a real man". Example: "We had to take away Henry's man card because he cried in public when Kristina dumped him". (urbandictionary.com)

In your group discuss what tasks you could add to a (stereo)typical "man card". Then think about your own ideas of manliness: What requirements does a man (not) have to meet to be a real man in your eyes?

EXTRA: Design a "lady card".

2. Watching the movie: Walt's masculinity

a. *Describe and analyze different aspects of Walt's masculinity throughout the film: What makes him a 'real man'? The grid below might help you to structure your findings.*

Actions/Deeds	Language	Symbols (actual objects)

b. *In your group, discuss which manly attributes you consider to be undesirable, although they are part of Walt Kowalski's positive image as tough guy and savior of the weak.*

3. Watching closely: Manning up Thao

a. *Walt teaches Thao how to speak and act like a man. Compare Thao's manliness before and after the lesson at the barber's. Closely watch chapter 18 (DVD 01:07:48 – 01:13:18/YouTube: Gran Torino (clip 11) "What do you want to do with your life, kid?") and 19 (DVD 01:13:19 – 01:16:46/YouTube: Gran Torino (clip 13) "He knows construction") again. Analyze how Thao's development is supported by the camera.*

	In the backyard	At the construction site
Content: the setting and Thao's actions (what image does this give him?)		
Language: how Thao speaks and reacts		
Camera angle		
Field size		
Conclusion		

b. *Compare your results in the group. Discuss Walt's role for Thao: teacher, friend, father? Something else?*

4. Exploring further: Femininity in Gran Torino

The movie revolves around two male protagonists, some critics have called it macho. Do you agree?

Sue is perhaps the only rounded character. From 1 to 10, how do you rate Sue's strength (1 = very weak, 10 extremely strong)? In your group compare your assessment and justify your point of view.

Is Sue a hero or a victim? Discuss her role in the film.

Task sheets for theme group: Gran Torino

1. Getting started: The significance of cars

"Cars are an extension of our personality. Cars really are another layer of clothing. Owning a car is like a rite of passage for most men."
"Men love cars because the better their cars look, the more manly they feel."
[Leslie Kendall, curator of Peterson Automotive Museum, Los Angeles]
"Most men love cars because the better their cars look, the more manly they feel." [Ahney Whitney Her, the actress who plays Sue in the movie]

The distinctive form of the Gran Torino Sport

a. *In your group discuss what these statements mean and if you personally agree. What role do cars play in your life and the life of your family and friends?*

b. *The Gran Torino (Sport) was a special version of the Ford Torino, an automobile which was produced in Detroit for the North American market between 1968 and 1976. The car was named after the city of Turin (Torino, in Italian), which was seen as "the Italian Detroit". The Gran Torino (Sport) was first produced in Detroit in 1972.*

Describe the car. Who do you expect to sit behind the wheel of such a car? Speculate about what role this car might play in the movie and why its name was chosen as the title of the movie.

2. Watching the movie: The role of Walt's Gran Torino

a. *Describe and analyze at least three scenes in which the Gran Torino plays a role. Use the table below.*

Action	Significance for Walt or Thao	EXTRA: Function of the scene for the movie

b. *"It's the Gran Torino that brings Walt and Thao together."*
In your group compare your results and discuss if you agree with this statement.

3. Watching closely: Looking after the Gran Torino

a. *Closely watch two short scenes again: Walt polishing his Gran Torino (DVD 00:22:28 – 00:23:19/YouTube: "Gran Torino, clip 4: Your number one son") and Thao inheriting the Gran Torino and driving away on Lake Shore Road (DVD: 01:45:26 – 01:46:29/"Gran Torino ending scene"). Describe and analyze Walt's relationship to his car in the first scene and its role as Walt's legacy in the second, final scene. Analyze the cinematic techniques that emphasize Walt's/Thao's emotions and their effect.*

	Scene 1: Walt and his Gran Torino	Scene 2: Thao inheriting Walt's legacy
Emotions		
Camera: (angle and field size)		
Colors/lighting		
Music (theme song: *Gran Torino*)		
Role/ significance of the Gran Torino		

b. *"The car is just a symbol of part of Walt. Walt sort of is the Gran Torino."*
   In your group compare and discuss your results and relate them to this quote by Clint Eastwood.

4. Exploring further: Movie cars

In your group make a list of movies where a car or other vehicle plays an important role. Discuss the function of the car for the movie. Does the car have a "personality"? Does it influence the plot in ways the characters do?

[TIP: The "Internet Movie Cars Database" has a good list of motor vehicles.]

That **Aston Martin**

Task sheets for theme group: Violence

1. Getting started: Violence starts with thoughts

> *"Nonviolence means avoiding not only external physical*
> *violence but also internal violence of spirit."*
> Martin Luther King Jr.

a. *In your group, explain the meaning of this quote. Describe the development of violent conflicts you know from your own experience, from the news or from literature and films.*

b. *Make a graph or chart which shows how a conflict ending in death might develop. You can use the pyramid and the phrases given. Work on your own, then compare the different versions within your group.*

intimidating – armed assault – pushing physically – attacking verbally – teasing / ridiculing sb's appearance or behavior – threatening – committing murder / suicide – standing in sb's way – ignoring and excluding sb – spreading rumours – physical assaults – harassment by groups – shoot out

2. Watching the movie: Escalating violence

a. *While watching, note down scenes that lead directly to or show increased violence. Use your results from task 1 to comment on the level of violence that is reached in each scene. Compare findings in the group.*

Characters involved	Violent behavior	Your comment

b. *Discuss what Walt could have done to prevent the conflict from escalating.*

3. Watching closely: Walt as a hero of violence

a. Re-watch the first part of chapter 7 (DVD: 00:23:20 – 00:25:46/YouTube: Gran Torino (clip 5 – part 1) "Get off my lawn"). Analyze the film techniques used to create atmosphere. Compare your findings in your group (word bank below!). Discuss other techniques that could have been used to create suspense.

Action	Atmosphere	Film techniques (camera movements, lighting, sounds/music)
The Hmong gang show up at the Van Lor's house and verbally put pressure on Thao to join their gang.		
Gang members violently force Thao to get into their car.		
Walt shows up and chases the intruders away, threatening them verbally and with his rifle.		

Word bank: tense, aggressive, turbulent, playful, gloomy (dark), cold, hostile, terrifying, threatening, merciless, alarming, chaotic, panicky, nervous, worried, lively, ambivalent, frantic, frightening, out of control

b. In your group discuss the validity of the following statements (at least two).
"The 'Get-off-my-lawn' scene ...
- ... is an urban version of a typical western."
- ... illustrates the US American belief in self-reliance and self-defense."
- ... turns Walt Kowalski into a hero of violence for the neighborhood."
- ... is one of the funniest scenes in the movie."
- ... is an example for the usefulness of the "Castle Law", which permits a homeowner to use deadly force to defend himself or herself against an intruder.

4. Exploring further: Representation of violence in films

Films are often mirrors of the culture that produces them. Discuss if and why Gran Torino can be seen as an expression of American concepts, beliefs and values – especially as related to the topic of violence.
Discuss what a German version of Gran Torino might look like.

Task sheets for theme group: Religion

1. Getting started: existential questions and religious symbols

a. *Explain the meaning of these two symbols (a candle and a cross) in Christianity. What role might they play in the movie?*

b. *In your group, think of existential questions that play a role in religion(s), e.g. "What is the meaning of life?" Discuss what questions and themes you expect to encounter in Gran Torino.*

_____

_____

_____

2. Watching the movie: References to the Christian faith

a. *Clint Eastwood's film is full of open and hidden references to the Christian religion. Note down the elements of Christianity that are shown in the movie (in chronological order). Summarize your findings for your group. Compare your results and discuss their significance.*

Phrase of film	Elements of Christianity
Beginning	
	1st *official confession in church*
	2nd *personal confession to Thao*
Ending	

b. *"Me I have got a light". Discuss the symbolism of light and the Christian cross (crucifix) in the movie.*

3. Watching closely: Walt's death

a. *Closely watch chapter 27 (DVD: 01:39:30 – 01:41:46/YouTube: "Gran Torino Walt Kowalski death scene") and describe the religious allusion in it. (Hint: stop the film when Walt is lying on the ground. Who does he resemble?) Analyze the film techniques used in Walt's final appearance and interpret their effect on the viewer. Focus on color and lighting, camera angle, field size and camera movement.*

	Description	Effect
Colors and lighting		
Camera angle		
Camera movement		
Field size		

b. *"Walt sacrifices himself to make up (atone) for his sins." Analyze this statement and discuss these sins.*

c. *Walt does not act according to conventional Christian wisdom – represented by Father Janovich – which teaches repentance ("confession") in Church followed by forgiveness for your sins. In your group discuss the two positions: Should you personally make up for your sins by (if you can) repairing what you have destroyed, or should your sins just be forgiven through Jesus the Savior, after a confession? Are there any other ways of repenting your faults and sins, in your opinion?*

4. Exploring further: Invisible religion

"Films and other media function as "invisible religion", says sociologist Thomas Luckmann. Just like traditional religions, they raise existential questions like: 'What is the meaning of life?', 'Is there a life after death?', 'How can we find forgiveness?' and 'What is good, what is evil?' And they offer answers to those questions to provide guidance and to make sense of our existence."

Discuss this theory, referring to other movies.

Excel in language: Prejudice and racism

1. Complete the grid by matching the given paraphrases with the words or phrases in the box below.

race riot – racist (noun) – racist (adjective) – race relations – racism – racial profiling – racial	

1.	way of behaving or thinking that shows you don't like or respect people from other races, and that you believe your race is better than any other one
2.	someone who does not like or respect people from other races, and who believes their race is better than any other one
3.	relating to racism (*rassistisch*)
4.	relating to race (*Rassen-*)
5.	the relationships between people of different races who live in the same community
6.	an occasion when people of different races who live in the same community fight violently against each other
7.	the practice of thinking that people of a particular race or colour will behave in a particular way, especially in a criminal way

2. Add the missing prepositions.

a. to discriminate _____ someone   *(jemanden benachteiligen)*

b. to feel discriminated _____ by someone   *(sich durch jemanden benachteiligt fühlen)*

c. to have prejudices _____ someone   *(Vorurteile haben gegenüber jemandem)*

d. to feel superior _____ someone   *(sich jemandem gegenüber überlegen fühlen)*

e. to feel inferior _____ someone   *(sich jemandem gegenüber unterlegen fühlen)*

Excel in language: Masculinity

1. *The words in the box are adjectives that are commonly – which does not necessarily mean suitably (!) – used to describe either femininity or masculinity. Make sure you understand what they mean before categorizing them into the grid. Add more adjectives if you can.*

> dependent, emotional, ambitious, aggressive, rebellious, accepting, submissive, self-confident, graceful, flirtatious, active, forceful, protective, individualistic, non-emotional, nurturing, tough-skinned, self-critical, competitive, passive, independent, sensitive, athletic, understanding, tender, dominant, vulnerable

Adjectives commonly associated with masculinity	Adjectives commonly associated with femininity

2. *Match the verb on the left to the collocations to get a list which describes (stereo)typical male behavior. Some verbs match more than one noun phrase.*

| to rise (rose, risen) – to offer – to take (took, taken) – to provide – to adopt – to demonstrate – to suppress – to use | sb protection *(jdm. Schutz gewähren)* – violence against sb *(Gewalt gegen jdn. anwenden)* – one's emotions *(seine Gefühle unterdrücken)* – to a challenge *(eine Herausforderung annehmen)* – safety to sb *(jdm. Sicherheit gewähren)* – revenge on sb *(sich an jdm. rächen)* – the father role for sb *(für jdn. die Vaterrolle annehmen)* – one's strength *(seine Stärke zeigen)* |

1. to rise to a challenge _____ 2. _____ 3. _____

4. _____ 5. _____ 6. _____

7. _____ 8. _____ 9. _____

10. _____ 11. _____ 12. _____

Excel in language: Gran Torino

1. *The following expressions are all taken from the movie. Write down their German equivalents. Add at least two more car expressions to the list. Use a dictionary to find the correct English translations.*

1. a vintage car	
2. a stunning/gorgeous/shiny car	
3. to be in mint/perfect condition	
4. to get into a car	
5. to slam the door	
6. to drive off in a car	
7. to screech the tires	
8. a vehicle pulls up to a place	
9. to hook a jumper cable to a dead battery	

2. *The verb 'to drive' (drove, driven) can have different meanings. Match the sentences with meanings.*

1. Do you promise to drive carefully?	To force someone to leave a place.
2. Stop driving yourself so hard.	To make someone extremely angry.
3. She drove him to the airport.	To control a vehicle (as a driver) carefully.
4. You're driving me up the wall.	To make someone work or try very hard.
5. They were driven out of their village.	To take someone to a place in a vehicle.

3. *A 'drive' is not necessarily a ride in a car. Find the other meanings of this noun in these sentences:*

a. *16500 Mulholland Drive, Los Angeles, CA* _____

b. *Insert the DVD into your disk drive.* _____

c. *She worked all weekend. She's full of drive and ambition.* _____

_____

d. *He didn't act rationally. He is totally controlled by his desires and drives.* _____

_____

Klett

Excel in language: Violence

Carefully go through these lists of collocations, looking up ones whose meaning or pronunciation you do not know for sure (e.g. www.macmillandictionary.com). Highlight and write in the table below the ones you think will be most helpful when talking about violence in Gran Torino.

ADJECTIVE + *VIOLENCE – Example: considerable violence –* considerable, great, excessive, extreme, large-scale, serious, continuing, escalating, growing, unnecessary, mindless, random, uncontrolled, brutal, criminal, unlawful, institutionalized, widespread, sporadic, domestic, physical, sexual, drug-related, communal, ethnic, racial, political, revolutionary, terrorist, left-wing, right-wing

VERB + *VIOLENCE – Example: engage in a conflict –* engage in, inflict violence on sb, resort to, turn to, suffer, provoke, denounce, deplore, hate, reject, breed (Hatred breeds violence), to quell the violence, be capable of (We're all capable of violence sometimes).

VIOLENCE + VERB *– Example: Violence broke out. –* break out, erupt, occur, escalate into, intensify, worsen, spread

VIOLENCE + PREPOSITION – against (violence against police officers), among (violence among football supporters), between (violence between rival ethnic groups), towards (violence towards ethnic minorities), within (violence within the family)

PHRASES – (punish) an act of violence, (call for) an end to violence, (be prepared for) an eruption/outbreak of violence, fear of violence, (live) a life of violence, (be prone to) outbursts of violence, a (downward) spiral of violence, a threat of violence, a victim of violence, a refuge for victims of domestic violence, violence breeds more violence, a wave of violence

Word / collocation	Meaning/pronunciation

Excel in language: Religion

This word bank might help you to talk about the movie and its religious themes.

> to deliver a eulogy – *eine Grabrede halten* • to repent/to show remorse for sth – *Reue zeigen* • to make atonement/to atone for a sin – *Sühne leisten für eine Sünde* • Christ crucified – *der gekreuzigte Christus*

The following expressions are all taken from the movie. Write down their German equivalents. Think of at least three more useful expressions related to religion. Use a dictionary to find English translations.

1. to go to confession	
2. to confess one's sins to sb/a priest	
3. to admit one's guilt	
4. to make amends	
5. to leave one's burden behind	
6. to absolve a person of his/her sins	
7. to reach one's salvation	
8. He would roll over in his grave if he saw that.	
9. the Our Father/Lord's Prayer	
10. "In the name of the Father, the Son and the Holy Spirit"	
11. to preach about life and death	
12. a (church) service	

© Ernst Klett Sprachen GmbH, Stuttgart 2017 | www.klett-sprachen.de | Alle Rechte vorbehalten.
Kopieren für den eigenen Unterrichtsgebrauch gestattet.
ISBN 978-3-12-577484-1

Theme group: Presentation

As a group prepare a presentation in which you share the results with the others. Summarize and visualize the main points on a poster or with a presentation program (PowerPoint, Keynote). You have 15 – 20 minutes to:

- Name your topic and comment briefly on it.

- Introduce about five to seven new words and phrases that you consider necessary or useful to talk about your topic. Write them onto the poster or a slide before the presentation so that you don't lose too much time. Make sure you know how to pronounce the words correctly (an online dictionary is the easiest way to find out, e.g. www.macmillandictionary.com, www.merriam-webster.com).

- Summarize the significance and context of your theme within the movie.

- When/how/how often does it occur? What message does it convey? What function does it have? What effects does it have on the viewer? What questions does it raise? What cinematic devices are used to draw the viewer's attention to it?

- Show one film scene (maximum: five minutes) or two shorter scenes (max. three minutes each) to illustrate your results. You can choose a scene you have worked on in your tasks or you can look for another scene and apply your insights to this new sequence.

Make sure that you split the speaking time evenly in your group.
Be well prepared so that you can speak freely and don't have to ask for words.

After your presentation your classmates will be able to ask questions. Your teacher might bring up questions and issues that you have discussed in your theme group.

Useful general words and phrases for presenting (and their meanings)

1. Starting your presentation "Today we're going to look at …"
2. The main points "Firstly: …; Secondly: … Next let's look at …"
3. Concluding "Finally, …" "In conclusion, …"

Theme groups: Wrapping up

While the other theme groups are presenting their results, work on the following tasks:

1. *Copy the words and phrases of each group into the table.*

2. *Gran Torino is a movie that deals with the big questions of American life. Use the theme web to note down these big questions as they are mirrored in the movie. Include insights from your own group work.*

3. *Find connections between the different themes. Visualize and verbalize them in the theme web.*

English word/phrase	Paraphrase/German translation

Gran Torino: Theme Web

Racism

Masculinity

Violence

Gran Torino

Religion

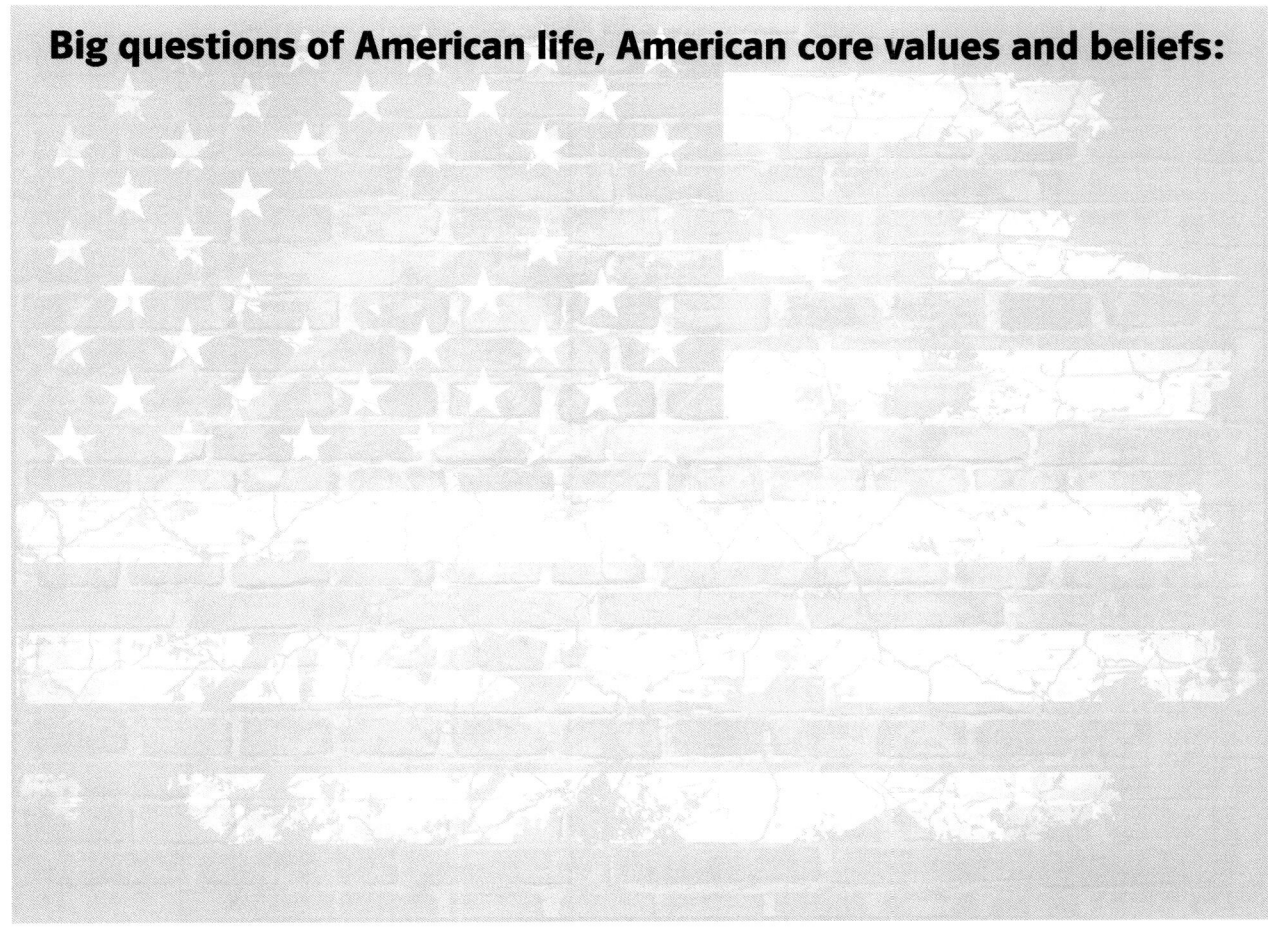

Big questions of American life, American core values and beliefs:

Klett

II Filmarbeit: Modul B: The Ambiguity of Belonging

Konzept

Mit diesem zweiten Unterrichtsmodul wird gezielt das Thema *The Ambiguity of Belonging* – literarisches Schwerpunktthema für Baden-Württemberg ab dem Schuljahr 2017/18 – in *Gran Torino* erarbeitet.

Die Tabellen geben einen Überblick über das umfangreiche Angebot an Arbeitsblättern und Methoden, welche die SuS für die Vielschichtigkeit des Themas sensibilisieren und sie zu einem vertieften Verständnis des Films führen. (Zeitangaben in Klammern beziehen sich jeweils auf die Dauer der Filmszene – 2:20 = 2 Minuten und 20 Sekunden).

Inhaltliche und sprachliche Hinführung zum Thema *The Ambiguity of Belonging* (ab hier: „A of B")

KV B1	Introduction: Identity and belonging (text A)	Introduction to the notions of identity and belonging.
KV B2	Introduction: Belonging as basic need (text B)	Introduction to Maslow's hierarchy of needs.
KV B3	A of B: Quotes	Various Quotes on "the sense of belonging".
KV B4	A of B: Ethnic minorities	YouTube clip: What kind of Asian are you? (2:20) Prejudices towards Asian-Americans.
KV B5	A of B: Language of belonging	Useful words and phrases to talk and write about the topic.

Analytische und kreative Aufgabenformate zu ausgewählten Szenen aus *Gran Torino*

KV B6	A of B: Character development	**While-viewing task** for the whole film: How Walt's and Thao's senses of belonging change.
KV B7	A of B: Opening sequence (12:39)	Walt's/Thao's sense of belonging to family/community.
KV B8	A of B: The gangs (4:42)	Thao and the two gangs: Thao's reluctance to join.
KV B9	A of B: Language (8:11)	The first barber scene and the "bro" scene: Different codes of belonging to a group.
KV B10	A of B: Walt's birthday (8:09)	Walt's birthday (his family then the Hmong family).
KV B11	A of B: Thao's initiations (6:40)	Thao's transition from childhood to manhood.
KV B12	A of B: Walt's confessions & atonement (4:19)	Walt's repentance and search for inner peace.
KV B13	A of B: Walt's will (6:22)	The significance of Walt's will for Walt and Thao.
KV B14	A of B: Walt's development	Overview of Walt's development.
KV B15	A of B: Thao's development	Overview of Thao's development.
KV K	Klausur	Vorschlag zur Leistungsüberprüfung.

Die Arbeitsblätter zum Film konzentrieren sich auf zentrale Szenen, die bis auf eine kleine Überschneidung noch nicht im Modul A analysiert wurden. Ihre Reihenfolge entspricht der Chronologie des Films. Inhaltlich bauen sie nicht aufeinander auf und können daher beliebig ausgewählt werden. Der Aufbau aller Arbeitsblätter zu den Filmszenen ist identisch:

1. Chunk box	Eine Aufstellung von Wörtern und Phrasen, die zum einen für das Verständnis, aber auch zur Beschreibung der Szene(n) hilfreich ist. Es werden möglichst frequente Phrasen aufgeführt, welche den aktiven Wortschatz der SuS differenzierter und reichhaltiger machen. Zudem wird das Augenmerk auf typische fehlerträchtige Strukturen gelenkt, um Fehler in der Sprachproduktion vorzubeugen. Wenn möglich, sind Wörter und Phrasen einsprachig umschrieben, wenn nötig ins Deutsche übersetzt.
2. Viewing/Reading comprehension	Geschlossene und halboffene Aufgabenformate zur Überprüfung des Hörseh-/ Leseverständnisses der Szene(n).
3. Analysis	Analytische Aufgabenstellung zur inhaltlichen Erarbeitung der Szene(n).
4. Analysis	Produktionsorientierte bzw. dramatische Aufgabenstellung zur inhaltlichen Vertiefung der Szene(n).
5. Conclusion	Zusammenfassung der Arbeitsergebnisse, die je nach Leistungsstand der SuS selbständig, individuell oder gemeinsam im Plenum angefertigt wird.

Organisation und Ablauf

Falls sich die SuS bereits durch die Projektarbeit von Modul A weitgehend eigenständig mit dem Film auseinandergesetzt haben, kann die Fokussierung auf das Schwerpunktthema im Anschluss erfolgen. **Unterrichten Sie aber lediglich das Modul B, empfiehlt es sich, die inhaltliche und sprachliche Hinführung zum Thema *The Ambiguity of Belonging* zumindest teilweise noch vor der Pre-viewing Phase und vor der Sichtung des Films einzuplanen.**

Eine **vollständige Präsentation** des Films im Unterricht ermöglicht den SuS ein authentisches Filmerleben und dient als Grundlage für die Analyse der Einzelszenen. Steht allen SuS der Film auch zuhause zur Verfügung (z. B. als DVD (ca. 5 EUR), als Amazon Video (ca. 8 EUR bzw. gratis in Amazon Prime), auf iTunes (ca. 8 EUR)), kann das Filmanschauen mit der While-Viewing Aufgabe (**KV B7**) in die HA verlegt und die Unterrichtszeit für die Szenenanalysen genutzt werden. Das Material eignet sich jedoch auch für einen step-by-step Ansatz.

Möglichkeiten und Empfehlungen zum Einsatz von Modulen A und/oder B)

Die Erarbeitung einer Szene kann in der Regel in einer Einzelstunde abgeschlossen werden. Die Analyseaufgaben („Watching closely") der Themengruppen *Prejudices and racism* und *Masculinity* und auch *Religion* überschneiden sich mit dem Schwerpunktthema *The Ambiguity of Belonging* und bieten sich deshalb bestens als Zusatzmaterial für Modul B an, falls die Projektarbeit nicht durchgeführt wurde. Auch die **Language Sheets** des Modul A können sehr gut zu einer Erweiterung des thematischen Wortschatzes der SuS herangezogen werden.
Alle Lösungen und Erwartungshorizonte zu diesem Modul finden Sie ab Seite 102.

Kommentare zu den Unterrichtsimpulsen und Kopiervorlagen

Auf der nächsten Seite ist eine Übersicht über die verschiedenen Ebenen und Aspekte des Themas, die nicht didaktisch aufbereitet ist und ggf. als Zusammenfassung zur Prüfungsvorbereitung benutzt werden kann.

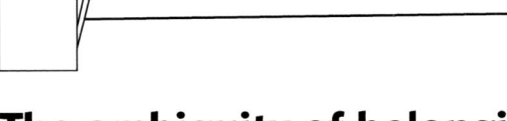

The ambiguity of belonging for:

1. The Hmong people
Geo-political ambiguity of belonging

The Hmong are an ethnic group from the hilly regions of China, Thailand, Vietnam and Laos. In the second half of the 20th century, the US Army recruited Hmong men from Laos to fight against the communists during the cold war. As a result, several hundred thousand Hmong people fled from Laos to Thailand as political refugees. Thousands of Hmong migrated to the West, mostly the US.

2. Thao
Social and cultural ambiguity of belonging

Thao is a second generation Hmong American, born in the US. He is a hybrid character, caught between Hmong and American cultures. His mother is more traditional, insisting on the Hmong way of life. He cannot identify with his cousin's Hmong gang. His father is absent, but described as "old school". This gap is filled by Walt, who teaches Thao aspects of the American way of life (working, how to communicate, dating, relying on oneself, etc).

Personal ambiguity of belonging: Family, groups, career, gender

Thao doesn't seem to fit in anywhere. He can't meet his family's expectations as the "man of the house" and refuses to join the Hmong gang. Before Walt helps him to "man up", he has no job. He is teased for his feminine looks and not being a "real man". The jobs he does are stereotypically seen as "women's work" – doing the dishes or gardening. Thao is usually a girl's name. He is an outsider with no close relationships – only Sue seems to understand him.

3. Walt
Social and cultural ambiguity of belonging

Walt no longer fits into "the old neighborhood", where he lives. He is one of the few white people left in a part of Detroit, which, in better days, used to be white and middle-class. His house sticks out among the run-down ones of his Hmong neighbors. He is like a fossil: the last survivor of an older generation of "real Americans" with "decent", conservative values. This is symbolized by the immaculate, deeply treasured Gran Torino in his garage. Also by his white Ford truck, which he drives around town, "saving the Helpless from the Wicked".

Personal ambiguity of belonging: Family, religion

Walt feels alienated from his own family. His two sons moved out with their families to a wealthy suburb (Grosse Point Park). They appear self-centered, greedy, disrespectful and superficial. Despite his racist attitudes towards his neighbors, he feels more closely connected to the traditional Hmong culture than to his "own" 21st century, decayed American one. The relationship to Thao and Sue becomes much closer and more caring than the one to his own sons has ever been. Walt shows his contempt for the church as an institution, but he develops a close relationship to Father Janovich. Walt feels burdened and alienated from himself. He did things in the past that do not match his personal beliefs and values: he killed people, even teenagers, in the war and feels he hasn't been a good father.

KV B1: Introduction: Identity and belonging (Text A); mit:

KV B2: Introduction: Belonging as a basic need (Text B)

Lernziele: Die SuS können einem Sachtext grundlegende Informationen und nützliche sprachliche Strukturen zur Identitätsbildung bzw. zu Maslows Bedürfnispyramide entnehmen und diese nutzen, um ihrem Partner eine dazugehörige Grafik zu erläutern. Sie können den Zusammenhang zwischen beiden psychologischen Theorien herstellen (und auf ihre eigenen Erfahrungen anwenden).

Ablauf: Jeweils zwei SuS lesen die beiden Texte arbeitsteilig in EA und tauschen sich im Anschluss in PA aus. Verständnisfragen und kritische Anmerkungen zu den Inhalten finden in einem abschließenden UG Raum.

Zusätzliche Aufgabenstellung: Mithilfe der Grafik auf KV B1 erstellen die SuS für sich selbst ihre persönliche Identity-Mindmap. Hier sollten die SuS selbst darüber entscheiden dürfen, ob sie diese teilweise sehr persönlichen Inhalte teilen wollen. Wichtig ist die Reflexion des Prozesses durch Fragen wie: *What difficulties did you have? Which aspects do you consider to be most influential? Can you think of other aspects that might influence your identity?*

KV B3: The Ambiguity of Belonging: Quotes

Lernziele: Die SuS können eine Vielzahl von Zitaten unterschiedlicher Persönlich-keiten zum Thema *belonging* verstehen, reflektieren und sich mit einem Partner über ihre persönliche Meinung und Erfahrung austauschen.

Ablauf: Die Teilaufgaben a., b. und c. werden jeweils in EA erledigt, bevor der Austausch in PA erfolgt. Die individuellen Ergebnisse können in UG nach jeder Teilaufgabe oder abschließend exemplarisch gesammelt und reflektiert werden.

Zusätzliche Aufgabenstellung: (für schnelle SuS): What different kinds of belonging can you identify in the quotes?

KV B4: The Ambiguity of Belonging: Ethnic minorities

Lernziele: Die SuS können beschreiben, was es bedeutet, einer bestimmten Nationalität zugehörig zu sein. Sie können einem kurzen Videoclip („What kind of Asian are you?") Informationen entnehmen und diese mithilfe einer Tabelle strukturieren und analysieren. Sie können sich in ethnische Minderheiten hineinversetzen, die im Alltag mit Vorurteilen und Fragen nationaler Zugehörigkeit konfrontiert werden. Sie können die im Video dargestellte Situation in den US auf die Situation in Deutschland übertragen.

Klett Online-Link:
99hdc98

Ablauf: Mit der Pre-Viewing Aufgabe im TPS Verfahren werden die SuS zum Thema *national identity* gelenkt. Die While-Viewing Aufgabe a. kann ein zweimaliges Anschauen des knapp 2½ minütigen Clips erfordern. Die ES erfolgt im Plenum und kann übergehen in die Diskussion der Aufgabe b. Als Post-Viewing stehen zwei Aufgaben zur Verfügung. Die erste kann zunächst in PA oder auch direkt im Plenum diskutiert werden. Die zweite Teilaufgabe ist umfangreicher und zeitintensiver und beinhaltet eine Textproduktion und -präsentation in PA.

Zusatzmaterial (für leistungsschwächere SuS): Der Trailer zum Dokumentarfilm "Where are you from from?" (auf vimeo verfügbar) zeigt die Problematik von Immigranten in Deutschland und in den USA auf, die zwischen zwei Kulturen stehen, ohne sich zu einer richtig zugehörig zu fühlen.

Online-Link:
9fy5yk4

KV B5: The Ambiguity of Belonging: Language of belonging

Lernziele: Die SuS können ihren thematischen Wortschatz erweitern, indem sie sich mit der idiomatischen Übertragung von Phrasen auseinandersetzen, Synonyme suchen und hilfreiche Chunks für ihren aktiven Sprachgebrauch auswählen.

Ablauf: Die Aufgaben werden am besten in EA erledigt und eignen sich daher auch gut als HA. Die ES kann durch Selbstkorrektur oder im Plenum erfolgen. Die Lösungen zu KV B5 sind auch im Schülerbuch.

KV B6: The Ambiguity of Belonging: Character development

Lernziele: Die SuS können die Entwicklung der beiden Protagonisten im Bezug auf ihr Zugehörigkeitsgefühl zu anderen visuell darstellen und analysieren.

Ablauf: Die SuS erstellen die Diagramme in EA während des Films oder direkt im Anschluss. Die Ergebnisse werden in einem abschließenden UG zusammengeführt.

KV B7: The Ambiguity of Belonging: Opening sequence

Lernziele: Die SuS können: eine Filmszene verstehen und ihr Informationen über die beiden Protagonisten entnehmen und diese strukturieren; Unterschiede und Gemeinsamkeiten zwischen Walt und Thao beschreiben und deren Zugehörigkeitsgefühl ihrem sozialen Umfeld gegenüber analysieren; sich in die Gefühlslage der Protagonisten hineinversetzen, indem sie eine Gedankenblase ausfüllen bzw. den Kontext einer Gedankenblase rekonstruieren; und die wichtigsten Erkenntnisse der Filmszenenanalyse zusammenfassen.

Ablauf: SuS werden aufgefordert, sich aktiv mit dem vorgegebenen Wortschatz der Chunk Box auseinanderzusetzen, indem sie beispielsweise Übersetzungen für Phrasen anfertigen, die einsprachig erklärt werden oder indem sie mit einer individuellen Markierungstechnik arbeiten: unterschiedliche Farben für besonders häufige und hilfreiche Phrasen, für bisher unbekannten Wortschatz und für besonders fehlerträchtige Strukturen (z. B. Präpositionen, schwierige Rechtschreibung etc). Die Hörsehverständnisüberprüfung erfolgt mit der ersten Sichtung der Szene. Die ES der geschlossenen oder halboffenen Aufgabe erfolgt im Plenum. Für die Analyseaufgabe 3 ist ggf. ein zweites Vorspielen der Szene notwendig. Die Erarbeitung der ersten Teilaufgabe erfolgt in EA, die ES im Plenum, dabei kommt es weniger auf eine vollständige Auflistung von Einzelbeobachtungen an, als auf die Zusammenfassung der Gemeinsamkeiten und Unterschiede. Die zweite Teilaufgabe wird im TPS Verfahren durchgeführt. Die produktionsorientierte Aufgabe 4 kann in PA oder einer kleinen Gruppe durchgeführt und durch eine Reflexion im Plenum abgeschlossen werden.

KV B8: The Ambiguity of Belonging: The gangs

Lernziele: Die SuS können eine Filmszene verstehen und mithilfe des Filmskripts verbale und non-verbale Überredungsstrategien der Hmong Gang analysieren und die Wirkung filmästhetischer Mittel erkennen. Sie können sich in Thao hineinversetzen, seine innere Zerrissenheit in einer kurzen Textproduktion zum Ausdruck bringen und diese reflektieren. Sie können die wichtigsten Erkenntnisse der Filmszenenanalyse zusammenfassen.

Ablauf: Umgang mit Aufgaben 1 und 2 (Chunk Box und Viewing Comprehension): siehe KV B7. Für Aufgabe 3 analysieren die SuS zunächst die rhetorischen Strategien von Smokie und Spider im Auszug des Filmskripts in EA (3a.). Die Analyse der Filmszene (3b) ergänzt die Ergebnisse um körpersprachliche Taktiken und untersucht die filmischen Mittel der Szene. Die ES der Teilaufgaben erfolgt jeweils im Plenum. In der kurzen Textproduktion in Aufgabe 4 versetzen sich die SuS in Thaos Lage und verschriftlichen seine ambivalenten Gedanken. Die Auswertung erfolgt in PA und einem zusammenführenden UG.

rhetorische Strategien

Alternative: Die Aufgabe kann auch mit der dramatischen Methode des „Thought tunnel" durchgeführt werden. Dazu bereitet die eine Hälfte der Klasse Argumente für das Beitreten in die Gang vor, die andere Hälfte Argumente dagegen. Anschließend bilden SuS einen Tunnel im Klassenzimmer, d.h. beide Hälften stehen sich in zwei Reihen mit etwa zwei Armlängen Abstand gegenüber. Je nach Gruppengröße melden sich zwei bis drei SuS freiwillig, um in die Rolle des Thao zu schlüpfen. Eine(r) dieser zwei oder drei SuS bleibt im Klassenzimmer, die anderen warten vor der Türe. Der/die S stellt sich an den Anfang des Tunnels, schließt seine Augen, versetzt sich in Thaos Situation und bewegt sich sehr langsam(!) vorwärts. Die außenstehenden SuS beginnen mit ihren Argumenten auf Thao einzureden, sobald dieser direkt vor ihnen ist. Argumente dürfen notfalls auch wiederholt werden, wichtig ist das eindringliche Einreden auf Thao. Ist Thao am Ende des Tunnels angelangt, darf er die Augen öffnen und sein Erlebnis reflektieren: *What feelings did this experience evoke?, Which side was stronger?, What's your decision?* Die Übung wird dann mit anderen „Thaos" durchgeführt und die Ergebnisse der einzelnen SuS verglichen und zusammengefasst.

„Thought tunnel"-Verfahren

KV B9: The Ambiguity of Belonging: Language

Lernziele: Die SuS können zwei kurze Filmszenen verstehen. Sie können herausarbeiten, wie in den beiden Szenen bestimmte Gruppenkonventionen ein Zugehörigkeitsgefühl schaffen und ihre Erkenntnisse mit ihren eigenen Erfahrungen in Bezug setzen. Sie können sich in Figuren hineinversetzen und deren Zugehörigkeitsgefühl mithilfe eines Standbildes zum Ausdruck bringen. Sie können die wichtigsten Erkenntnisse der Filmszenenanalyse zusammenfassen.

Ablauf: Umgang mit Aufgaben 1 und 2 (Chunk Box und Viewing Comprehension) siehe „Ablauf" für KV B7 auf Seite 54.

Für die Analyse in Aufgabe 3 ist ein zweites Vorspielen der Szenen erforderlich. Die wichtigsten Ergebnisse werden im Plenum zusammengetragen und dienen als Grundlage für die weiterführende Diskussion von 3b und c in PA, die in einem abschließenden UG münden kann. Aufgabe 4 stellt zunächst einen Sprechanlass dar, da sich die SuS in der Gruppe auf einen bestimmten Moment einigen und die Befindlichkeit der jeweiligen Figuren beschreiben müssen. Die SuS werden aufgefordert, einen Perspektivwechsel vorzunehmen und die Gefühlslage der Charaktere körpersprachlich zum Ausdruck zu bringen. Die „Animation" des Standbildes durch eine Bewegung und einen Satz führt zum einen zu einer intensiveren Auseinandersetzung mit dem Filmmoment, erfordert eine zusätzliche Abstimmung innerhalb der Gruppe und macht zudem die Präsentation sehr viel interessanter und fruchtbarer. Die Präsentation kann zentral oder aber dezentral durchgeführt werden, indem jeweils 2–3 Gruppen zusammengehen. Mögliche Beobachtungsaufträge für die zuschauenden SuS können sein: *Describe the position of every single character and their relationship to each other in detail;*

Identify the moment: Describe the setting and the context of the freeze frame;
Sense of belonging or non-belonging? What does the freeze frame express? How is
this effect created?

KV B10: The Ambiguity of Belonging: Walt's birthday

Lernziele: Die SuS können eine Filmssequenz verstehen (und die Bedeutung eines
englischen Sprichworts erklären und dieses auf die Filmszene beziehen). Sie
können das Gefühl der Einsamkeit des Protagonisten im Verlaufe der Sequenz in
einem Diagramm visualisieren und beschreiben und Walts Sinneswandel erklären.
Sie können die Symbolik der Spiegelszene mithilfe von Deutungsvorschlägen
interpretieren und in einem Schreibauftrag Walts Selbstgespräch ausführen.
Sie können die wichtigsten Erkenntnisse der Filmszenenanalyse zusammenfassen.
Ablauf: Umgang mit Aufgaben 1 und 2 (Chunk Box und Viewing Comprehension)
siehe „Ablauf" für KV B7 auf Seite 54.
Für die Analyse der Aufgaben 3 und 4 ist ggf. ein zweites Vorspielen der Szenen
erforderlich. Alle Teilaufgaben von 3 sowie 4a können im TPS Verfahren durchgeführt werden. Falls die Auswertung der Textproduktion durch eine Präsentation
erfolgen soll, muss zusätzliche Zeit für das Einüben des Vortragens eingeplant
werden. Ansonsten kann eine inhaltliche und sprachliche Rückmeldung zur
Textproduktion durch die L oder MitschülerInnen erfolgen.
Zusätzliche Aufgabe aus Modul A, die zu dieser Szene hinführt: KV A1, (*Prejudices
and Racism*), Aufgabe 3 „Watching Closely".

KV B11: The Ambiguity of Belonging: Thao's initiations

Lernziele: Die SuS können drei kurze Szenen in ihren Kontext einbetten und Thaos
Initiationsriten im Film erkennen. Sie können Thaos Einführung in die „Männer-
sprache" beschreiben und diese auf ihre Funktion hin analysieren. Sie können
Thaos Schritte ins Erwachsenwerden skizzieren und über kulturelle Unterschiede
des Mannseins reflektieren. Sie können die wichtigsten Erkenntnisse der
Filmszenenanalyse zusammenfassen.
Ablauf: Umgang mit Aufgabe 1 (Chunk Box) siehe „Ablauf" für KV B7 auf Seite 54.
Vor dem Vorspielen der „manning up" Sequenz erfolgt eine
Leseverständnisüberprüfung, bei der die SuS jeweils den Kontext der kurzen
Skriptauszüge beschreiben und Thaos unterschiedliche Übergangsriten im Film
benennen. Aufgabe 3a ist eine Hörsehverständnisüberprüfung, die bereits zur
Analyse der Szene hinführt. Die ES kann zunächst in PA oder aber direkt im Plenum
erfolgen. Für Aufgabe 4 müssen die SuS ihre Erkenntnisse aus der Szenenanalyse
auf den Film ausweiten und Thaos Entwicklungsschritte in die Zugehörigkeit zur
(amerikanischen Männerwelt) skizzieren. Die zu erwartenden unterschiedlichen
Ergebnisse der einzelnen SuS bieten einen motivierenden Redeanlass, der durch
die Diskussionsfrage 4c in der Gruppe oder im Plenum inhaltlich vertieft werden
kann.
Zusätzliche Aufgabe aus Modul A, die zu dieser Szene hinführt: KV A2 (*Masculinity*),
Aufgabe 3 *Watching Closely.*

KV B12: The Ambiguity of Belonging: Walt's confessions & atonement

Lernziele: Die SuS können eine Filmsequenz inhaltlich verstehen und Parallelen zwischen zwei Szenen erkennen. Sie können die Gründe für Walts Handeln mithilfe von Deutungsvorschlägen interpretieren und Walts Wiedergutmachung seiner Fehler in der Vergangenheit durch seinen Märtyrertod analysieren. Die SuS können in einem kreativen Schreibauftrag Walts innere Entwicklung sowie die Beweggründe für seine Selbstaufopferung transparent machen. Sie können die wichtigsten Erkenntnisse der Filmszenenanalyse zusammenfassen.

Ablauf: Umgang mit Aufgaben 1 und 2 (Chunk Box und Viewing Comprehension) siehe „Ablauf" für KV B7 auf Seite 54, dabei geht 2b bereits in die Analyse. Aufgabe 3 und 4 gehen beide über die Szene hinaus und können nur bearbeitet werden, wenn die SuS Walts Todesszene kennen. Aufgabe 3a bietet einen Diskussionspunkt, der sich für eine PA oder ein UG eignet. 3b wurde durch Aufgabe 2 vorbereitet und analysiert Walts persönliche Art der „Sühne" (Sühne durch Selbstaufopferung als logische Konsequenz seines Glaubens an Selbstjustiz). Die ES sollte im Plenum erfolgen. Für die kurze Textproduktion in Aufgabe 4, welche einem „dritten Geständnis" ähnelt, versetzen sich die SuS in Walts Lage und verschriftlichen die Gedanken des wortkargen Mannes, der wenig über seine Gefühle spricht. Die inhaltliche und sprachliche Rückmeldung zur Textproduktion kann durch die L oder MitschülerInnen erfolgen.

Zusätzliche Aufgabe aus Modul A. Sie analysiert die Todesszene und bietet eine Ergänzung dieser Szenenanalyse: KV A5 (*Religion*), Aufgabe 3 *Watching Closely*.

KV B13: The Ambiguity of Belonging: Walt's will

Lernziele: Die SuS können eine Filmsequenz verstehen. Sie können den Stellenwert von Figuren innerhalb einer Figurenkonstellation beschreiben und analysieren. Sie können die unterstützende Wirkung von Filmtechniken (auch der *dissolve* als besondere Form des Editings) analysieren. Sie können Thaos Gemütslage in der Abschlussszene beschreiben und deren filmästhetische Umsetzung deuten. Sie können die wichtigsten Erkenntnisse der Filmszenenanalyse zusammenfassen.

Ablauf: Umgang mit Aufgaben 1 und 2 (Chunk Box und Viewing Comprehension): siehe „Ablauf" für KV B7 auf Seite 54.

Die Notarszene muss für die Bearbeitung der Aufgabe 3 mindestens ein zweites oder auch ein drittes Mal vorgespielt werden. 3a wird in EA erledigt und vor der Diskussion von 3b im Plenum besprochen. 3c erfordert wieder eine individuelle Erarbeitung mit abschließender exemplarischer Auswertung im Plenum.

Die zusätzliche Aufgabe stellt ein differenzierendes Angebot für besonders schnelle oder leistungsstarke SuS dar. Die Ergebnisse der Analyseaufgabe 4a werden von den SuS graphisch dargestellt und bieten in der Auswertung einen geeigneten Redeanlass in PA oder im UG. 4b lenkt den Fokus abschließend auf kinematografische Mittel, die das Zusammengehörigkeitsgefühl der beiden Protagonisten evozieren (im TPS-Verfahren oder direkt im UG zu erarbeiten).

KV B14: The Ambiguity of Belonging: Walt's development;

KV B15: The Ambiguity of Belonging: Thao's development

Lernziele: Die SuS können die Entwicklung der beiden Protagonisten im Hinblick auf *The Ambiguity of Belonging* zusammenfassen.

Ablauf: Die Teilaufgaben können je nach Angaben bzw. je nach Bedarf in EA, PA oder im UG erarbeitet und ausgewertet werden.

Leistungsbewertung

Klausur KV:
Seiten 90–91.
Erwartungshorizonte:
Seiten 109–110.

Für die Leistungsmessung steht **eine Klausur** zur Verfügung (KV "K"), in der die in diesem Modul erarbeiteten Inhalte und sprachlichen Strukturen sowie die geschulten Kompetenzen überprüft werden. Die Länge der Klausur entspricht einer Abiturklausur. Für eine 90-minütige Klausur wird nur <u>eine</u> der beiden Textproduktionen gestellt: die *Analysis*, die direkt an die Filmszene der Hörsehversehensaufgabe anknüpft oder die *Composition*, welche sich losgelöst von der Filmszene auf den ganzen Film bezieht. Die Gesamtpunktzahl kann bei 60 VP belassen werden, wenn der Inhalt der Textproduktion 20 VP und die Sprache der Textproduktion 30 VP zählen. Soll das Hörsehverstehen mehr Gewicht bekommen ergibt sich eine Gesamtpunktzahl von 45 Punkten.

Introduction: Identity and belonging (text A)

a. *Get together with a partner. You each have a different text. When you have finished reading, explain the graphic below to your partner, based on the information you have read. As you read, note phrases you can use.*

b. *After your presentations, summarize together how the two texts are related.*

> Your identity defines who you are. Your sense of identity and belonging is influenced by numerous factors, including your experiences, relationships and your environment. Finding your identity and belonging can be hard since we are challenged by the questions who we are, who the others want us to be and where we belong. No one can answer these questions for us. It is our personal view that
> 5 influences our decisions. Identity is multifaceted since your identity is shaped by a combination of different traits. You do not only possess one specific identity but may change your own identity depending on the environment and the people that surround you. For example, you may be extrovert with your family but rather reserved and serious with your school friends. You may speak a different language (e.g. different vocabulary and intonation) with your parents than with you soccer team. We
> 10 adjust our identity in order to fulfil our desire to belong.
> Here are some facets of our identity:
> **personal:** personality traits, qualities, skills, appearance, gender; **family:** role in the family; **career:** profession; **social:** social class, community, peer group, co-workers, clubs, gang; **ethnic/religious:** race, traditions, language, religion; **national:** origin and place of residence, language; **cultural:** ethnicity,
> 15 religion, history
> Everything and everyone can influence a person's identity and belonging. For different people, the same experience may affect them completely differently. Although we all live in the same world where many of our experiences overlap, the reason why we are all unique is because we ultimately choose what does or does not impact us in a crucial or unimportant way.

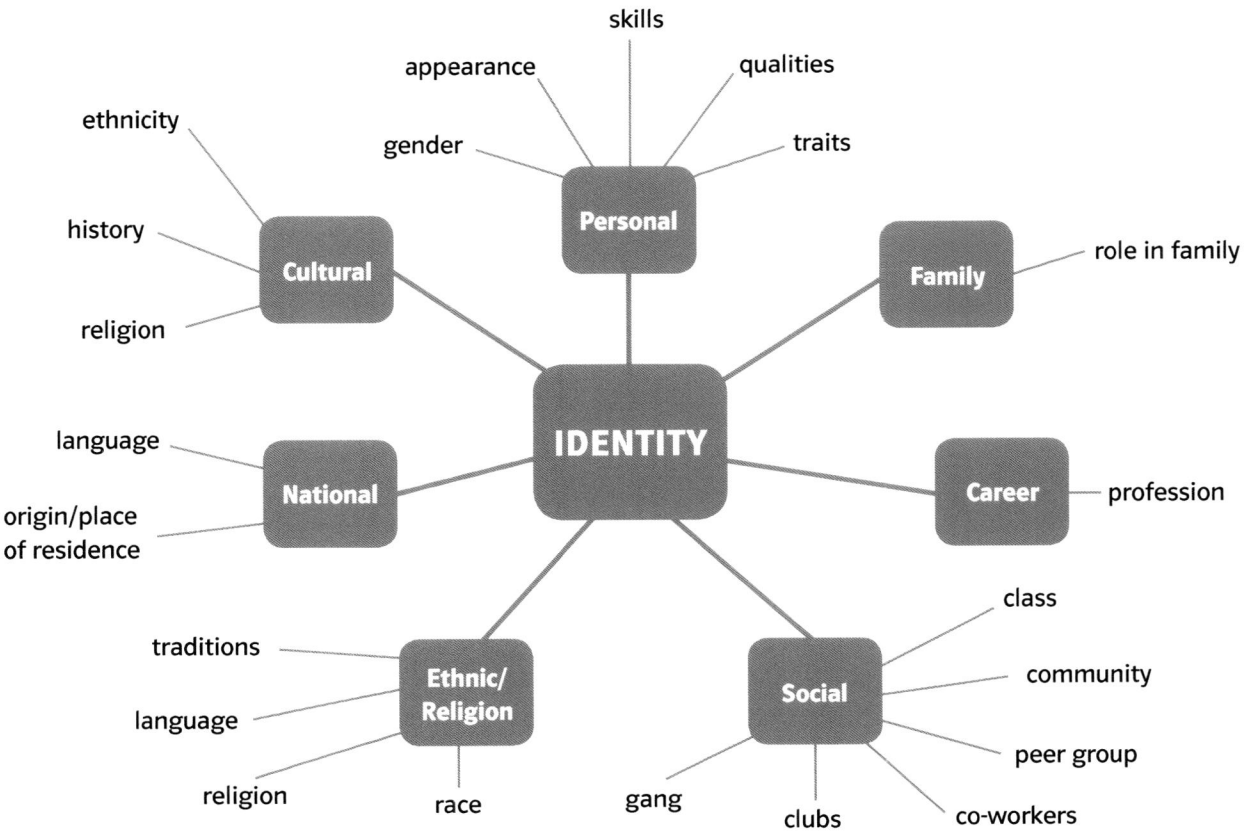

Introduction: Belonging as basic need (text B)

a. *Get together with a partner. You each have a different text. When you have finished reading, explain the graphic below to your partner, based on the information you have read. As you read, note phrases you can use.*

b. *After your presentations, summarize together how the two texts are related.*

Abraham Maslow (1908–1970) was an American psychologist best known for his 'hierarchy of needs', a psychological theory centered on our inborn desire for fulfillment. His levels of basic needs are often represented in a pyramid. The theory states that a person does not feel the second need until the demands of the first have been met, nor the third until the second is met, and so on. Here are Maslow's needs:

5   **1. Physiological Needs**
These are biological needs for oxygen, food, water and warmth. They are the strongest needs because they come first in a person's search for satisfaction.

2. Safety Needs
With all physiological needs satisfied, those for security become active in unstable times or emergency.

10 **3. Needs for Love, Affection and Belongingness**
The next class that emerges consist of the needs for love, affection and belongingness. There are many different forms of belonging: relationships (e.g. family, friends, partners, pets), social groups (e.g. classes, clubs, gangs, church, co-workers, organisations, communities) and environments (e.g. nation, race, region, city, culture). Many people become susceptible to loneliness or even depression if they lack a sense of belonging.

15 **4. Needs for Esteem**
When the first three classes of needs are satisfied, the needs for esteem can become dominant. These involve needs for both self-esteem and for the esteem a person gets from others. Humans have a need for a stable, high level of self-respect, and respect from others. When these needs are satisfied, the person feels self-confident and valuable as a person in the world. When these needs are frustrated, the person feels inferior, weak, helpless
20 and worthless.

5. Needs for Self-Actualization
When all of the foregoing needs are satisfied, then and only then are the needs for self-actualization activated. Maslow describes self-actualization as a person's need to be and do that which the person was "born to do." "A musician must make music, an artist must paint, and a poet must write."

The Ambiguity of Belonging: Quotes

> *"I don't even remember the season. I just remember walking between them and feeling for the first time that I belonged somewhere."*
> **Stephen Chbosky, in: The Perks of Being a Wallflower**

a. Make a sketch of the image the quote evokes for you. Who are "I" and "they"? What might be the reason for the speaker's feeling of belonging? Compare your results with your neighbor(s).

b. Reflect on your own experiences: When do you have the feeling that you belong (to a person, to a group, to a community, to a nation), and why? Share your thoughts with your partner.

c. Read the quotes below and mark the ones that appeal to you most. Discuss your choice with your partner.

> *"You can search high and low to find happiness on earth, yet unless you love yourself, you will never find your true belonging."*
> **Leon Brown, author**

> *"A sense of belonging is not physical. We can't find it by changing where we live or what we do. We have to carry it within us."*
> **Phyllis C. Cast, author**

> *"Happiness, I think, has to come in the beginning, truly, from feeling a sense of well-being within yourself.*
> *To me it's that incredible sense of belonging and peace within your own self and heart that really is joy."*
> **Goldie Hawn, actress and film producer**

> *"We know that where community exists it confers upon its members identity, a sense of belonging, and a measure of security. ... Communities are the ground-level generators and preservers of values and ethical systems".*
> **John Gardner, author**

> *"A deep sense of love and belonging is an irreducible need of all people. We are biologically, cognitively, physically, and spiritually wired to love, to be loved, and to belong. When those needs are not met, we don't function as we were meant to. We break. We fall apart. We numb. We ache. We hurt others. We get sick."*
> **Brené Brown, author**

> *"The dynamism of any diverse community depends not only on the diversity itself but on promoting a sense of belonging among those who formerly would have been considered and felt themselves outsiders."*
> **Sonia Sotomayor, Associate Justice of the Supreme Court of the US**

The Ambiguity of Belonging: Ethnic minorities

1. Pre-viewing: Belonging to Germany

What defines a person's "Germanness"? Rank the criteria, indicating which are the most important and least important to you. Add more if you want. Compare and discuss your result with your neighbour.

- The person was born in Germany.
- The person lives in Germany permanently.
- The person works and pays taxes in Germany.
- German is the person's mother tongue.

- The person's outer appearance does not reveal that (s)he belongs to a different ethnic group.
- The person has assimilated to German traditions and habits.

2. While-viewing: Prejudices

a. *Watch the video clip "What kind of Asian are you?" Outline both the man's assumptions about the woman and the actual facts.*

The man's assumptions about the woman	Actual facts about the woman

b. *Explain what the clip criticizes in a humorous way.*

3. Post-viewing: The ambiguity of belonging

a. *Assess how realistic/exaggerated the video clip is. What effect do such everyday experiences have on the sense of belonging of ethnic minorities (e.g. Asian-Americans, African-Americans, Latino-Americans) in the US?*

b. *Discuss if and how you could make a similar video about Germany. Write a dialogue for such a clip. Be prepared to act it out for the class or to make a short film.*

The Ambiguity of Belonging: Language of belonging

1. *Look at the German meanings of the two single words 'ambiguity' and 'belonging'. Come up with some idiomatic translations for the phrase 'the ambiguity of belonging'. It does not have to be a word by word translation.*

Ambiguity:
Ambiguität
Ambivalenz
Doppelbödigkeit
Doppeldeutigkeit
Doppelsinn
Doppelsinnigkeit
Mangelnde Eindeutigkeit
Mehrdeutigkeit
Unbestimmtheit
Uneindeutigkeit
Unklarheit
Vieldeutigkeitkeit
Zweideutigkeit

Belonging: Zugehörigkeit

The Ambiguity of Belonging: **Translations**

2.

> "There is a reason why the word 'belonging' has a synonym for 'want' at its center; it is the human condition."
> *Jodi Picoult*

Solve the riddle: What is the center of the word 'belonging' which is a synonym for 'want'?
Look the word up in a good collocation dictionary and find prepositions, adjectives and verbs that go with the word.

3. *In the list of 18 words, find eight synonyms for 'ambiguity' and eight for 'belonging'. Two words do not fit in.*

incertitude – kinship – vagueness – affinity – double meaning – transition –
uncertainty – attachment – loyalty – relationship – doubtfulness – challenge – enigma –
obscurity – inclusion – unclearness – acceptance – association

Ambiguity ~ _____

_____

_____

_____

Belonging ~ _____

_____

_____

_____

4. *Complete the grid by writing the German translation into the right-hand column. Add at least two more verbs that are useful to talk about the idea of belonging or not belonging. Write at least five sentences about the characters in Gran Torino using different verbs from the list.*

Verb + complement	Examples	Translation
to belong (somewhere)	*Please put the books where they belong! / This is the place I belong.*	
to belong to somebody	*Who does this car belong to?*	
to belong to something	*She belongs to the local film club.*	
to belong to somebody/ something	*He belongs to Mr. Bennet's group, not mine.*	
to feel a sense/have a feeling of belonging	*At church, I finally felt a strong sense of belonging.*	
to join sth	*He joined the chess club in 2015.*	
to join sb for sth	*Would you like to join us for dinner?*	
to identify with sth	*He can't identify with their beliefs.*	
to participate in sth	*She agreed to participate in the meeting.*	
to take part in sth	*They refused to take part in the discussion.*	
to be/feel part of sth	*Joe felt like part of the family.*	
to exclude sb from sth	*They excluded him from the meeting.*	
to be/feel excluded from sth/sb	*She felt excluded from the agreement.*	

<u>Sentences:</u>

a. _____

b. _____

c. _____

d. _____

e. _____

5. *Go through these words and phrases. Write down those not yet in your active vocabulary. Use a dictionary!*

share everything with sb – long to belong – do the right thing – have friends –
be part of a community – trust in sb – have confidence in – happiness – rely on sb –
feel respected by sb – be free to be oneself – form a team – be different but the same –
(not) be judged – group acceptance – feel connected – be a part of sth – join a group –
give/receive hugs – have a place to go (to) – everyone is different – hope – care for sb –
be at ease – feel comfortable/secure/safe/included – group member – organization – club –
association – similar – alike – control – be suitable – fit in – ethnicity – boundaries – be related to –
a strong/close bond – establish a connection with – play together – work together – laughter –
one of a kind – be accepted for who you are – stand out – have sb on your side –
mutual understanding – togetherness – support each other – assist each other –
have sympathy for sb – show undivided loyalty to sb – partnership – feel included/excluded –
be close to sb – feel responsible for sb – look after sb – be committed to sb – sacrifice oneself for sb –
share (the) responsibility for sth

The Ambiguity of Belonging: Character development

1. Walt's belongingness

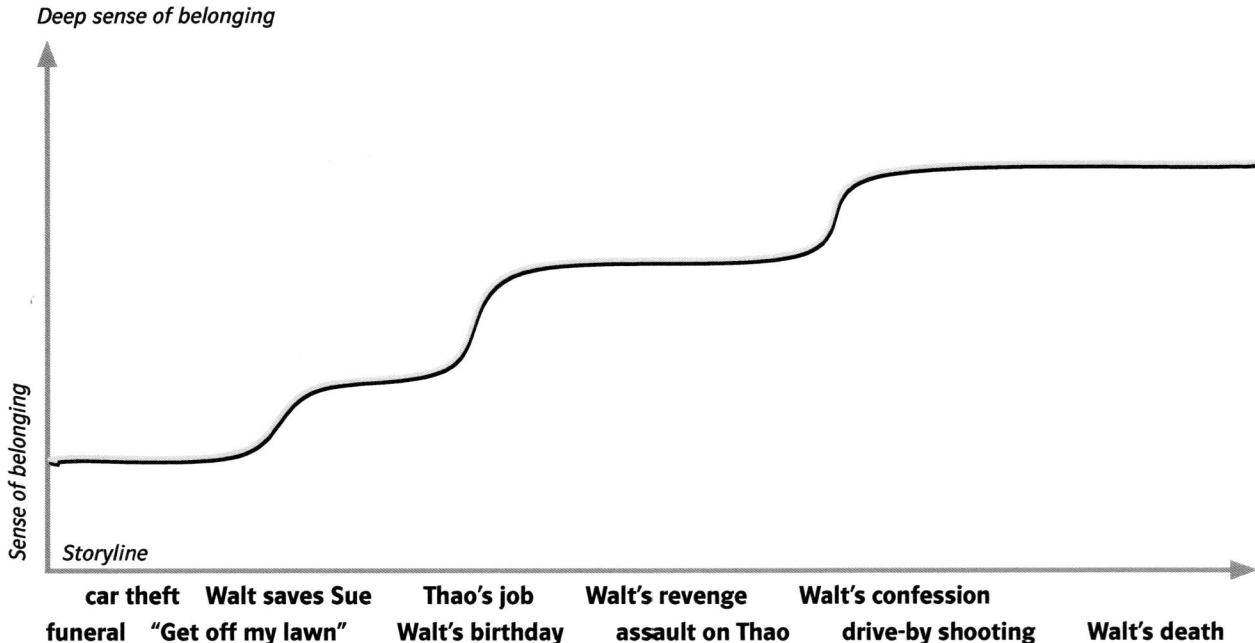

Deep sense of belonging

Sense of belonging

Storyline

car theft   Walt saves Sue   Thao's job   Walt's revenge   Walt's confession

funeral   "Get off my lawn"   Walt's birthday   assault on Thao   drive-by shooting   Walt's death

The line illustrates how Walt's sense of belonging towards Sue changes in the course of the movie. Use different colors to show: Walt's feeling of belonging towards: his sons (red); Thao (blue); and the priest (green). Compare and discuss results with your neighbor. Assess what the diagram tells you about Walt Kowalski.

2. Thao's belongingness

Draw a diagram for Thao, illustrating his sense of belonging towards Sue, his family and Walt. Compare and discuss results with your neighbor. Assess what the diagram tells you about Thao.

Deep sense of belonging

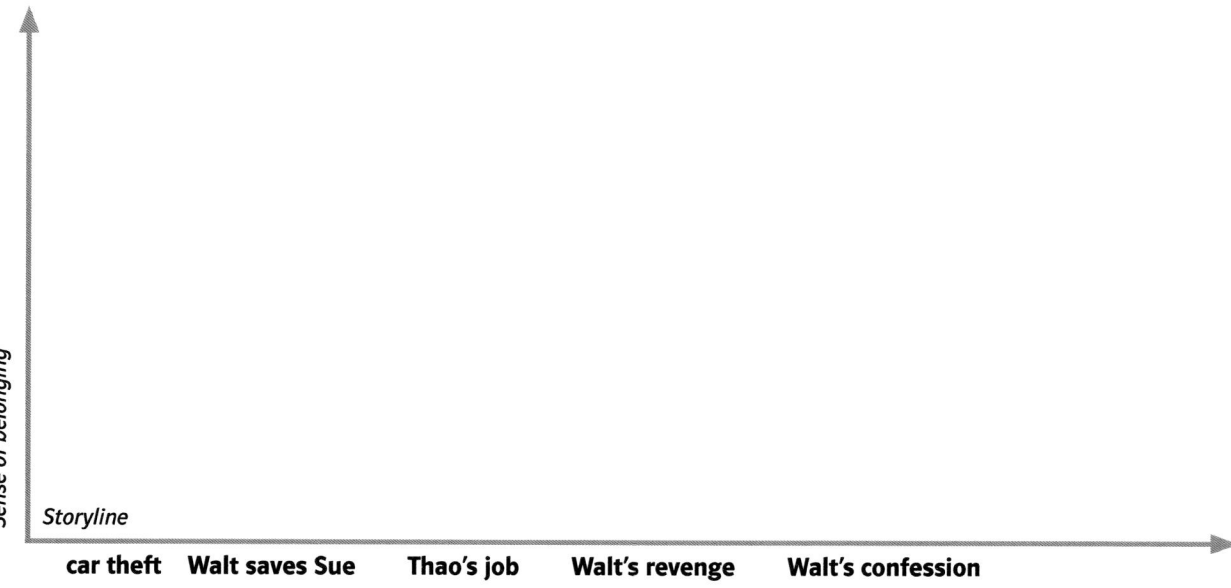

Sense of belonging

Storyline

car theft   Walt saves Sue   Thao's job   Walt's revenge   Walt's confession

funeral   "Get off my lawn"   Walt's birthday   assault on Thao   drive-by shooting   Walt's death

Klett

The Ambiguity of Belonging: Opening sequence (00:00:00 – 00:12:39)

1. Chunk box

> **to attend a funeral service** to take part in a religious ceremony when sb has died – **to deliver/give a eulogy** to give a speech at a funeral about the person who has died – **to act in a disrespectful, impolite way** opposite of to act in a respectful and polite way – **to feel contempt for sb, to despise sb** to dislike and have no respect for sb – **to gather at a funeral reception** to come together somewhere to talk and eat after a funeral – **jumper cables** electrical wires to connect batteries of two cars if one battery is dead – **to mourn (for sb)** to feel sad that sb has died and to express this in public – **to go to confession, confess your sins** to admit in church to a priest that you have done evil, and you ask for forgiveness – **to have a birth ceremony** to perform ritual acts for a newborn baby – **to (not) feel at ease** to feel (un)comfortable – **to be submissive** to be willing to do what other people tell you to do without arguing or disputing

2. Viewing comprehension

Complete the following sentences.

a. The Kowalski family is in church because ... _____

b. The sons are worried about their father because ... _____

c. Walt does not want any help from his son or his granddaughter since ... _____

d. When the grandsons sneak around in Walt's basement they find ... _____

e. The priest asks Walt to come to confession because ... _____

f. Walt feels bothered by Thao because ... _____

g. In the garage Ashley asks Walt for two things: ... _____

h. Walt shows deep contempt for his Hmong neighbors by calling them ... _____

i. The Hmong have a family gathering in order to ... _____

3. Analysis: Walt and Thao in their families

a. *The two protagonists, Walt Kowalski and Thao van Lor, are introduced in the context of their families and friends. Note and compare what you learn about them in this opening sequence.*

Finally, summarize any obvious similarities and differences between these two male protagonists.

	Walt	**Thao**
Description of their family (outer appearance, behavior)		
Religious traditions/ceremonies and their reactions towards them		
Behavior/actions: what they say and do		
How the others see them		
How they seem to feel		
Similarities		
Differences		

© Ernst Klett Sprachen GmbH, Stuttgart 2017 | www.klett-sprachen.de | Alle Rechte vorbehalten.
Kopieren für den eigenen Unterrichtsgebrauch gestattet.
ISBN 978-3-12-577484-1

Klett

b. *Decide where to place each protagonist on a scale of 1 to 10. "1" means a very strong feeling of alienation from family and community; "10" means: very deep sense of belonging towards family/community.*
Compare results and justify your choices. Discuss reasons for the protagonists' behavior and states of mind.

Walt:

1 --- 5 --- 10

Thao:

1 --- 5 --- 10

4. Analysis: Slipping into someone's skin

Find a partner. One focuses on Walt, the other on Thao. Pick a moment from the sequence that is especially emotional for your character. Write down his thoughts in the thought bubble (circa 50 words). Afterwards, exchange texts and guess which moment your partner picked. Discuss why you each chose this exact moment.

> **Useful words:** upset – disappointed – sad – frustrated – humiliated – proud – ashamed – desperate – anxious – frightened – furious – shocked – worried – nervous

5. Conclusion: Their sense of belonging

Walt's sense of belonging	Thao's sense of belonging

Summarize Walt's and Thao's respective senses of belonging as expressed in this first sequence.

The Ambiguity of Belonging: The gangs (00:12:40 – 00:17:21)

1. Chunk box

> **to harass sb (verbally/sexually)** to keep annoying sb in an offensive and intrusive way – **to offend sb, to be offensive towards sb** to insult sb, to hurt sb's feeling(s) – **to fly solo** *(slang)* ⟷ **to be tight with sb** to be on your own and not belong to a group – **"we're coz"** *(slang)* we're cousins, we're family – **to convince sb to do sth** to talk to sb about sth so they believe it's right *(überzeugen)* – **to persuade sb to do sth** to talk sb into doing sth although it's maybe wrong *(überreden)* – **to possess great power of persuasion** to have the ability to persuade or convince sb – **in mint condition (e.g. a car)** in excellent shape, looks like new

2. Viewing comprehension

Tick the correct statements. Only one statement in each sentence is correct.

1. The Mexican gang members offend Thao by

- ☐ laughing at his typically Asian features.
- ☐ making fun of his name (a girl's).
- ☐ teasing him for being as short and light as a girl.
- ☐ ridiculing him for his feminine looks.

2. After chasing the Mexican gang, the Hmong gang tries to persuade Thao to get in the car

- ☐ by offering him money.
- ☐ by threatening to kill him with the gun.
- ☐ by saying that he must be thankful for their help.
- ☐ by promising him a girlfriend.

3. When the Hmong gang shows at the house,

- ☐ we find out how old Sue is.
- ☐ we learn what Spider's real name is.
- ☐ we get that Smokie is Thao's cousin.
- ☐ we realise that Thao is already 18.

Klett

3. Analysis: The gang's powers of persuasion

a. *Read the film dialogue closely. Analyze the verbal strategies the gang uses to persuade Thao to join them.*

SMOKIE	Hey, you wanna roll with us, man?
SPIDER	Dude.
SMOKIE	Come on, ride with us. Come on.
SPIDER	Come on, chill with us. You need somebody to protect you, man. That's what your big coz is for.
SMOKIE	Look, dawg. I been there, and I seen it, man. Back in the day, everybody used to wanna beat me up, dawg. But now look. Nobody wanna fuck with me. Come on, let's go.

SPIDER	We're coz, right?
SMOKIE	Come on.
SPIDER	We're coz, right? We're family.
SMOKIE	Look, a brother to Spider is a brother to me. Come on.
SPIDER	Dude man, take this shit off. Come on.
SMOKIE	Come on, roll with us. Come on.
SPIDER	That's a woman's work.
SMOKIE	Come get your hands dirty, man.

[**dawg** – (*slang*) close friend]

b. *Re-watch the scene (00:16:06 – 0:16:42). How do Spider/Smokie use their bodies to put pressure on Thao?*

c. *Analyze the effects of camera angles/field size that underline the verbal and physical pressure Thao feels.*

Camera technique	Effect
Camera angle	
Field size	
Other techniques	

4. Analysis: Thao's ambivalence

a. *Thao is torn between "flying solo" and "rolling with the gang". Imagine two voices in his head. Make a list of reasons for i) staying away from them, and ii) joining them.*

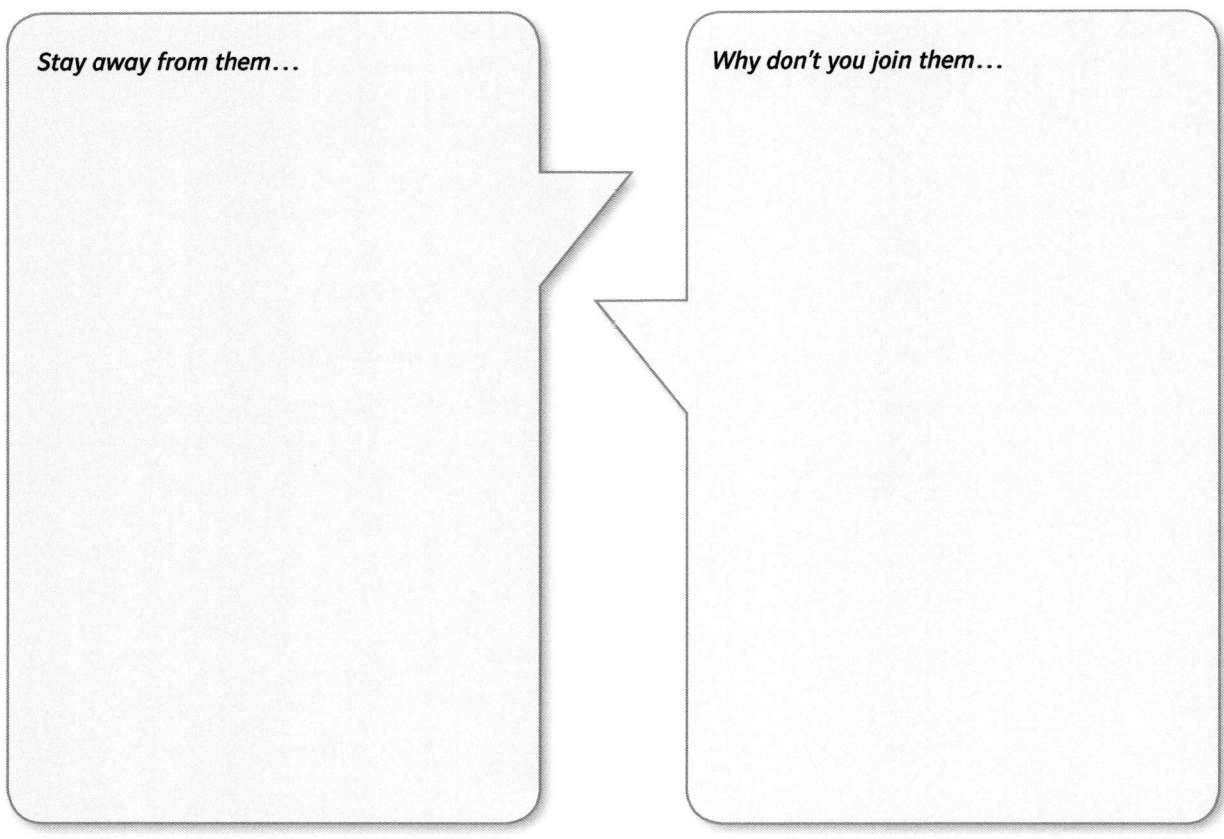

Stay away from them...

Why don't you join them...

b. *Compare your ideas with a partner and decide which voice is stronger.*

5. Conclusion: Thao's lack of belonging

Explain why Thao is an ideal "victim" for a gang (just like many other young Hmong men).

_____

_____

_____

_____

_____

_____

_____

_____

_____

_____

© Ernst Klett Sprachen GmbH, Stuttgart 2017 | www.klett-sprachen.de | Alle Rechte vorbehalten.
Kopieren für den eigenen Unterrichtsgebrauch gestattet.
ISBN 978-3-12-577484-1

Klett

The Ambiguity of Belonging: Language   (00:30:22 – 00:38:33)

1. Chunk box

> **to banter (with sb)** to tease/make fun of each other in an affectionate way – **a cheap person** sb who is unwilling to spend money – **a prick** *(offensive/vulgar)* highly insulting word for a man (prick = *Penis*) – **hard-nosed** uncompromising, tough – **to keep the change** *das Wechselgeld behalten* – **to hang out in a bad/unsafe neighborhood** *sich in einem schlechten/unsicheren Viertel rumtreiben* – **mouthy** rude, impolite – **to keep sb on the leash** *jdn an der Leine führen* – **to put a chain/chains on sb** *jdn anketten* – **to yank sb** to pull sb suddenly with force – **to quit doing sth** to stop doing sth – **spook** *(offensive and racist)* offensive hate word for a black person – **to come across sb** to meet sb by chance – **wrinkles, wrinkly** *(Haut)falten, faltig* – **"Shut your face!"** *(informal)* "Halt die Schnauze!"

2. Viewing comprehension

a. Scene 1: At the barber's

Tick the correct sentence(s). Correct the wrong one(s).

1. Martin says Walt should come more often because his haircuts are really cheap.   ☐

_____

2. Walt says he waits so long for haircuts as he hopes a more competent barber
    will finally replace Martin.   ☐

_____

3. Five years ago Walt used to pay 10 dollars for a haircut.   ☐

_____

4. Walt says that he won't wait for three weeks to get his next haircut.   ☐

_____

b. Scene 2: At the street corner

Put the statements into the correct chronological order. One statement is incorrect and must be crossed out.

_____ Sue is not intimidated, bravely defends herself.   _____ The gang acts in a defensive way.

_____ The gang feels provoked and threatens Trey.   _____ Trey courageously tries to protect Sue.

_____ The gang ridicules Walt because of his age.   _____ One of the African-Americans sexually
                                                                                    harasses Sue with words and gestures.

_____ The gang doesn't know how to deal with Sue
and becomes physically aggressive.   _____ Trey pretends to be one of the gang members.

3. Analysis: Signs of belonging (00:30:43 – 00:34:36)

a. *Watch the two scenes closely. Analyze the conventions or "codes" used that establish a sense of belonging to a group (e.g. dress code, specific language, gestures). In each scene, 1 <u>and</u> 2, focus on:*

	scene 1: **Walt and Martin**	scene 2: **The African-American gang members**
Note down similarities in the outer appearance, body language and gestures between the people		
Note phrases and describe the language that the people use to show that they belong to a person or a group		
What does this "code" reveal about the kind of relationship the people have?		

b. *Compare your results with your own experience: Do you also share different languages or codes with certain people or groups, which underline your sense of belonging to them?*

4. Analysis: Freeze frames

Find a partner (or two). Pick a moment from the sequence that you think expresses "belonging" or "not-belonging" especially well. Then:

1. *Prepare a freeze frame to capture this moment.*

2. *Animate your freeze frame: Each student develops one gesture or movement out of his or her position.*

3. *In a last step add a short sentence to your gesture.*

Present your portrayal in three steps:

1. freeze frame; 2. freeze frame+movement; 3. freeze frame + movement + sound

5. Conclusion: Sense of belonging

Summarize the influence of language and other "codes" on our sense of belonging or lack thereof.

_____

_____

_____

_____

_____

_____

_____

_____

_____

_____

_____

_____

_____

_____

_____

_____

_____

The Ambiguity of Belonging: Walt's birthday   (00:38:34 – 00:46:43)

1. Chunk box

> **1. She drops her grocery bags. 2. "Can we just drop it?"** 1. She lets her grocery bags fall on the ground.
> 2. "Can we just stop doing it/talking about it?" – **to maintain sth (a house/a vehicle/a road)** to keep sth in a
> good condition (by repairing it) – **to mow the lawn** to cut grass (in a yard or a park) – **to shovel snow** to use
> a shovel to remove snow from a pathway – **to be alert** to be able to think in a clear way – **to benefit from
> (doing) sth** to profit from (doing) sth – **old people's home, retirement home** *Altersheim, Seniorenheim* – **"I'm
> (just) kidding."** *(colloquial)* "I'm not serious!"/"I don't mean it seriously!" – **After all, it is** my birthday.
> *Immerhin/schließlich habe ich Geburtstag.* – **to yell at sb, to be yelled at** to shout at sb, to be shouted at – **to
> express embarrassment** to show that you feel embarrassed *(peinlich)* – **to come back for seconds** to come
> back to help oneself to more food – **a shaman** [ˈʃɑːmən] a priest-like person who can cure illnesses – **to have
> no flavor** to not taste like anything – **gook** very offensive word for sb from Asia

2. Viewing comprehension

Take notes to answer the following questions. Make two points for each question.

1. What does Walt's horoscope say?

_____

_____

2. Why does Walt get so angry at Mitch and Karen's presents and suggestions?

_____

_____

3. What arguments does Sue use to persuade Walt to come over to the barbecue?

_____

_____

4. What Hmong rules of conduct (i.e. rules of how to behave) does Walt learn from Sue?

_____

_____

5. What does Kor Khue, the shaman, "read" in Walt?

_____

_____

EXTRA: With a partner, agree on a German translation for the proverb "When in Rome, do as the Romans do."
Explain its meaning (possibly with examples of your own experience) and relate it to the barbeque scene.

3. Analysis: "Happy Birthday"

a. *Make a "graph of loneliness" for Walt. Discuss your results with your neighbour, justify your assessment.*

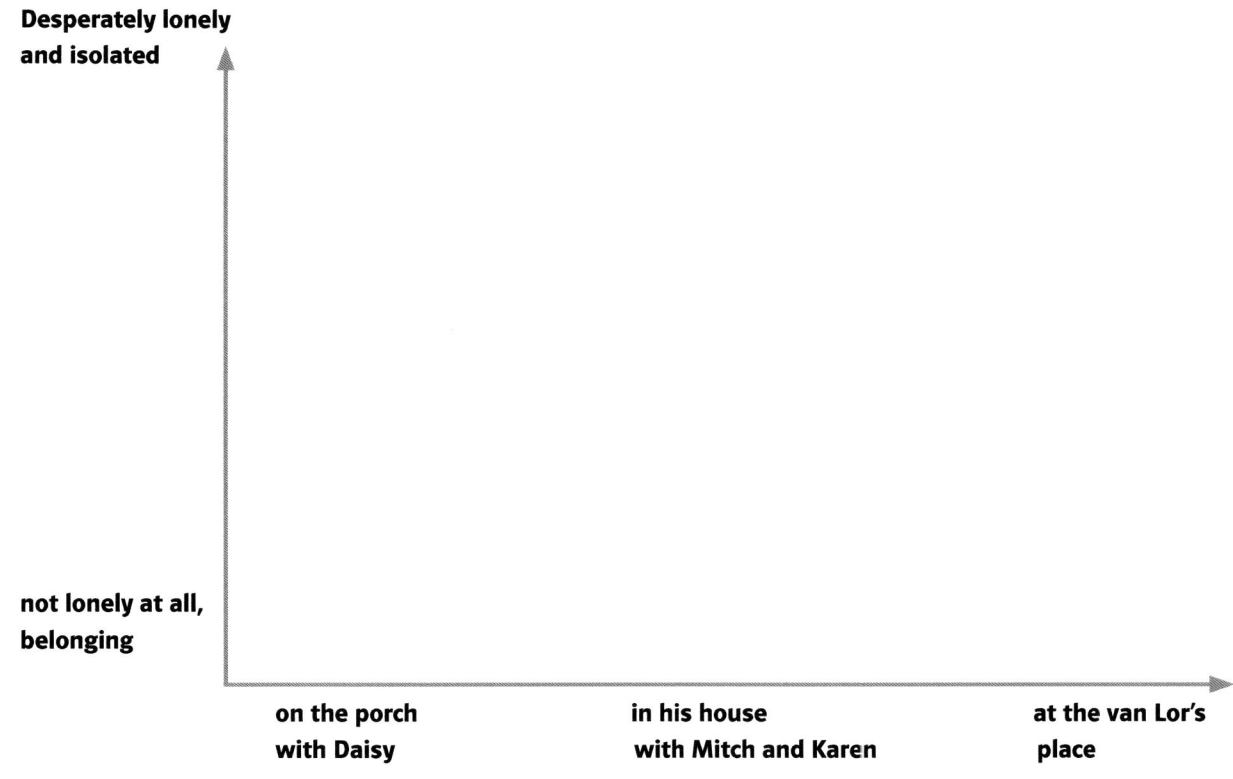

Desperately lonely and isolated

not lonely at all, belonging

on the porch with Daisy   in his house with Mitch and Karen   at the van Lor's place

b. *Analyze Walt's change of heart on his birthday when he overcomes his prejudices against the Hmong "barbarians". Why does he suddenly respect/admire them? Think of these elements and their relationships:*

Sue   The shaman   The Hmong people

WALT

Thao   Food/drinks

4. Analysis: The mirror moment

> *And since you know you cannot see yourself*
> *So well as by reflection, I your glass*
> *Will modestly discover to yourself*
> *That of yourself which you yet know not of.*
>
> **William Shakespeare, Julius Caesar, Act I, scene 2**

a. The mirror is a widespread symbol in literature and film. It can be a symbol of:

- physical reflection, showing how we currently appear;
- inner reflection and self-evaluation, reflecting upon our thoughts and our identity;
- a character's duality (dark/bright side);
- prophecy foreshadowing the future.

Discuss what meaning(s) the mirror has in Walt's mirror scene.

b. *Write an extension of Walt's mirror moment, in which he reflects on his birthday, explaining his new insights.*

_____

_____

_____

_____

> "God, I've got more in common with these gooks than I have with my own spoilt, rotten family. Jesus Christ …
> Happy Birthday."

_____

_____

_____

_____

_____

_____

5. Conclusion: Sense of belonging

Assess Walt's growing sense of alienation to his family and growing sense of belonging to the Hmong people.

_____

_____

_____

_____

_____

_____

The Ambiguity of Belonging: Thao's initiations   (01:10:06 – 01:16:46)

1. Chunk box

initiation process or ceremony in which sb becomes accepted by a group or society – **rite of passage** ceremony or event that marks a decisive stage in sb's life, e.g. becoming an adult or member of a religious group, etc. – **zipperhead** *(offensive)* highly offensive word for sb from Asia, which may go back to the Korean war, when US jeeps ran over Asian enemy soldiers. The tires sometimes left patterns that looked like a zipper *(Reißverschluss)* on the dead bodies. – **toad** 1. *Kröte* 2. Offensive word for a stupid person – **to blow sth** *(informal)* etwas vermasseln – **to gather sth** here: to think/assume sth – **to talk sb into doing sth** to persuade sb to do sth – **to banter (back and forth) with sb** to speak in a playful and teasing way with sb – **to vouch for sb/sth** *für jdn/etwas bürgen/einstehen* – **to be totally/really into (doing) sth** to like (doing) sth and be convinced of it – **You bet!** *(spoken)* Of course! – **You owe me one!** *(spoken) Du schuldest mir was!*

2. Reading comprehension

a. *Read the texts and locate them. Find their setting, context, what happened before and what will happen next.*

Text 1
GRAND: I'm just so broken-hearted. I want my daughter to find another husband. If she married again, there would be a man in the house.
MAN: What about Thao? The man of the house is right there.
GRAND: Look at him washing dishes. He does whatever his sister orders him to do. How could he ever become the man of the house?
MAN: Be patient, once he's older, he will be the man of the house.
GRAND: No way.

Text 3
WALT: So… what exactly was the deal with those guys out on my lawn that night? Who are they?
THAO: A gang. Hmong gangbangers.
WALT: I gathered that. What did they want with you?
THAO: They wanted to take me away because I blew my first initiation.
WALT: You joined up with those pukes? Damn, you are a pussy. Why in the hell did you do that?
THAO: I don't know. They were persuasive. My cousin's in the gang. They just talked me into it I guess.
WALT: Well, at least you're honest about it. So how'd you blow your first initiation?
Thao nods towards the Gran Torino.
WALT: The Gran Torino?
Thao nods. Walt laughs.
WALT: Christ all Friday.

Text 2
WALT: Relax, zipperhead. I am not gonna shoot you. I'd look down too if I was you. You know, I knew you were a dipshit the first time I ever saw you. You're worse with women than you are with stealing cars, Toad.
THAO: Thao.
WALT: What?
THAO: It's not toad, it's Thao. My name is Thao.
WALT: You were blowing it with that girl who was there. Not that I give two shits about you, Toad.
THAO: You don't know what you are talking about.
WALT: You are wrong, egg roll. I know exactly what I am talking about. I may not be the most pleasant person to be around. But I got the best woman who was ever on this planet to marry me. I had to work at it. That was the best thing that ever happened to me. Hands down. But you … you know. You let Click Clack, Ding Dong and Charlie Chan just walk out with what's-her-face. She likes you, you know. Though I don't know why.
THAO: Who?
WALT: Yum Yum! You know that girl in the purple sweater. She's been looking at you all day, stupid.
THAO: Do you mean, Youa?
WALT: Yeah, Yum Yum. Yeah. Nice girl, very charming girl. I talked with her. But you let her just walk right out. With the three stooges. And you know why? Cause you are big, fat pussy. Well …I gotta go. Good day. Puss cake.

b. *Thao failed the first gang initiation (stealing the Gran Torino). What might Thao's next initiations be?*

3. Analysis: The language test (01:10:06 – 01:15:38)

a. *Watch the two scenes with Walt and Thao, first at the barber's shop and then at Mr. Kennedy's office. Use the grid to take notes on the rules Walt teaches Thao in the first scene and tick off (b) the ones that Thao actually follows in the second scene. Analyze your findings: Has Thao passed the test?*

How to talk like real men:

Do's	Don'ts

b. *Their language is full of extremely offensive, racist, vulgar expressions. Give some examples and explain why the friends deliberately use such offensive language (they obviously do not intend to insult each other).*

4. Analysis: From Toad to Thao

a. *From dishwasher to owner of a Gran Torino. Make four snapshots to illustrate Thao's steps towards manhood. If you don't like drawing, write short descriptions of the snapshots.*

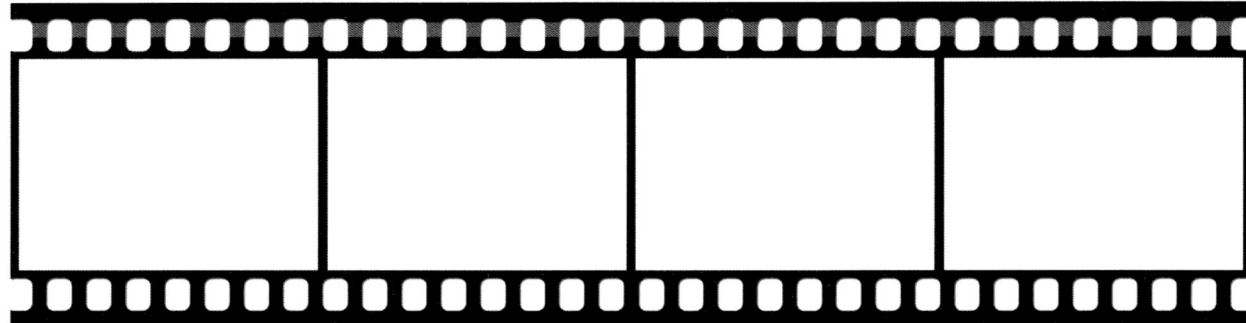

b. *Swap results with a partner, who should identify the scenes. Compare and justify your choices.*

c. *Discuss whether Walt's initiation into manhood for Thao has been successful and if manliness means the same for Americans and for the Hmong. Has he finally become "the man of the house" of the Hmong family, a role his grandmother did not consider him capable of at the beginning of the movie?*

5. Conclusion: Sense of belonging

Summarize Thao's development and his ambivalence of standing in between boyhood and manhood.

_____

_____

_____

_____

The Ambiguity of Belonging:
Walt's confession & atonement

(01:32:33 – 01:37:25)

1. Chunk box

> **to go to confession** *zur Beichte gehen* – **to absolve sb from one's sins** *jdn von seinen Sünden freisprechen* – **to make amends for sth** *etwas wiedergutmachen* – **to atone for one's sins** *für seine Sünden büßen* – **as atonement for sth** *als Wiedergutmachung für etwas* – **a confessional with a latticed window** *ein Beichtstuhl mit einem Gitterfenster* – **to retaliate against sb for sth** *sich bei jdn für etwas rächen* – **Not a day goes by that I don't think about it.** *Kein Tag vergeht, an dem ich nicht daran denke.* – **to lock sb up in the basement** *jdn im Keller einschließen* – **to be soiled** *to be unclean, here: to have sinned* – **We've come a long way.** We have achieved many things – **You've got your whole life ahead of you.** *Du hast dein ganze Leben vor dir.*

EXTRA: Explain the use of the present perfect in these sentences.

"What have you done?"	"How long has it been since your last confession?"
"Bless me, Father, for I have sinned."	"It's bothered me most of my life."

What tense do you expect Walt to use in his confession? Why?

2. Viewing comprehension

Take notes. What does Walt confess to Father Janovich in church and to Thao in the basement?

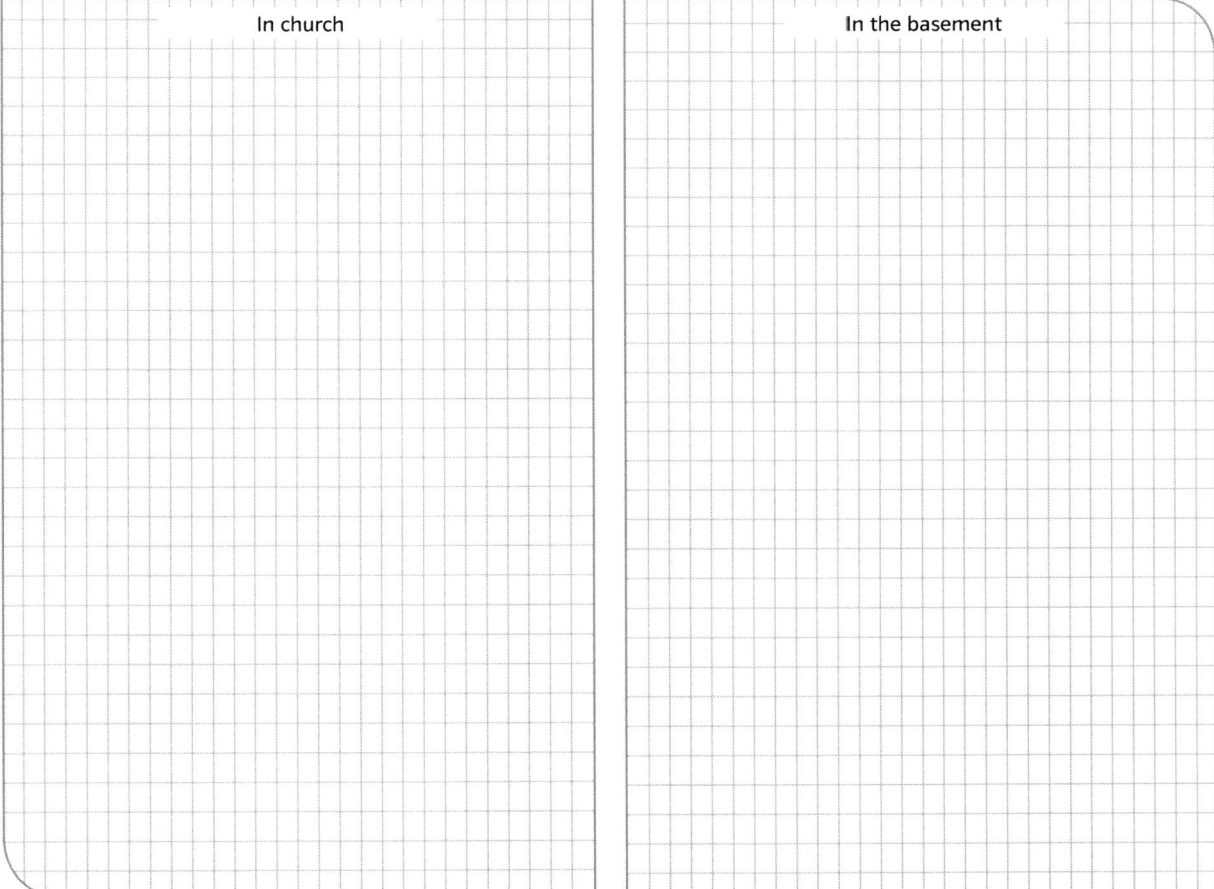

In church

In the basement

EXTRA: Compare the content, the setting and the characters in the two confessions.

3. Analysis

a. *Which statement(s) do you agree with? Which do you disagree with? Point out your strongest arguments.*

Walt goes to confession because:

1. ... it had been his wife's wish.
2. ... he has regained confidence in the church through Father Janovich.
3. ... he seeks forgiveness for his sins through Jesus Christ.

_____

_____

_____

b. "The thing that haunts a man the most is what he <u>isn't</u> ordered to do." *(Walt to Father Janovich)*

Explain Walt's statement. Outline how he finally makes up (atones) for these past mistakes:

Past mistakes that burden Walt	How Walt makes up for them in the movie
i) He has never had a close relationship with his sons.	
ii) He killed a teenager in Korea, although he had surrendered.	
iii) He intensified the gang conflict, including the drive-by shooting and Sue's brutal rape.	

4. Analysis: Being at peace

> "He says: 'You have no happiness in your life. It's like you are not at peace.'" *(Sue translating the Shaman's words for Walt)*… "I am at peace." *(Walt to Father Janovich after his confession)*

a. Explain what it means (not) "to be at peace". You can refer to your own experience.

b. Imagine Walt writes a note to Thao and Sue on the day he dies. He tells them how their friendship has finally brought him peace and light and explains his plan to defeat the Hmong gang to them. Write this note.

5. Conclusion: Sense of belonging

Outline Walt's development towards a feeling of belonging in the sense of self-acceptance and inner peace.

The Ambiguity of Belonging: Walt's will   (01:45:25 – 01:51:47)

1. Chunk box

> **to deliver/give a eulogy** to give a speech at a funeral about the person who died – **to make/write a (last) will (and testament)** to create a legal document that states what you want to happen to your money and belongings after you die – **to leave sb sth/to bequeath** [brˈkwiːθ] **sth/to hand down sth to sb** to (say that you) leave sb sth after your death – **to inherit sth from sb** to receive sth from sb who has died – **to receive an inheritance from sb** to get money or possessions from sb who has died – **to leave sb a legacy** *ein (materielles oder ideelles) Erbe hinterlassen* – **cultural heritage** traditions and beliefs that are part of the history and culture of a group – **along the lakeshore** following the banks/shore of a lake – **to sit in the passenger seat** to sit in the front seat next to the driver – **to head for/to** to go in a certain direction or to a certain place – **Where are you headed?** Where are you going? What's your destination? – **lighthouse** tower with a flashing light that tells ships where they are

2. Viewing comprehension

a. *Walt leaves his Gran Torino to Thao in his will, but only conditionally. Name at least two of the conditions.*

_____

_____

_____

_____

_____

b. *Choose the best adjective(s) to describe Walt's language from the notary's point of view (left side) and from Thao's point of view (right side). EXTRA: Justify and explain your assessment.*

Notary		Thao
☐	ironic	☐
☐	formal	☐
☐	offensive	☐
☐	intimate	☐
☐	vulgar	☐

_____

_____

_____

_____

_____

_____

Klett

3. Analysis: Walt's last will and testament

a. Rank the characters present at the notary in order of status (in relation to everyone else). Who has (or _thinks_ they have) the highest/lowest status (from 1–6) at the <u>beginning</u> and who at the <u>end</u>? Explain your choices.

	Beginning	End
Notary	☐	☐
Thao van Lor	☐	☐
Mitch Kowalski (Walt's oldest son)	☐	☐
Karen Kowalski (Mitch's wife)	☐	☐
Ashley Kowalski (Mitch and Karen's daughter)	☐	☐
Steve Kowalski (Walt's younger son)	☐	☐

b. Discuss what kind of ranking or hierarchy this is. Does the status depend on the character's ethnicity, social class, profession, age or maybe something else?

c. Analyze the film techniques used to emphasize the change in Thao's ranking (e.g. picture composition (where is he positioned?); lighting; field size; other aspects).

– Composition   _____

_____

– Lighting   _____

_____

– Field size   _____

_____

EXTRA: One aspect of _post-production editing_ is putting the different shots and sequences of the movie together, called _cutting_. The most common cut is the _hard cut_, where one shot ends and the next one starts immediately. But the transition from the notary scene to the final Gran Torino scene is made with a _dissolve_. Watch this transition (cut) at least twice. Describe what a _dissolve_ is and what function it has (why did the editor NOT choose a hard cut?). Stop in the middle of the dissolve and analyze the effect it produces.

Description	Function	Effect

4. Analysis: Gentle now a tender breeze blows

a. Describe Thao's state of mind in the final scene. Which emotions do you consider to be most dominant?

sad – loved – confused – optimistic – alone – self-confident – safe – proud – in the right place

Visualize your findings by creating a hand-written "wordle", in which the size of the letters indicates the intensity of the feeling. You can find numerous examples of wordles on the internet (picture search).

b. In the scene there is a strong sense of belonging between Walt and Thao, even though Walt is dead. Analyze the techniques used to emphasize the bond between these two unusual friends. What symbols are used? What effect does the music (mood, voice) have?

c. Read quotes from Jamie Cullen's theme song "Gran Torino" and/or listen to it. The bittersweet ballad, sung by Clint Eastwood, revolves around themes from the movie.

*"So tenderly your story is
nothing more than what you see
or what you've done or will become."*

*"standing strong do you belong
in your skin; just wondering."*

*"Gentle now a tender breeze blows
whispers through the Gran Torino
whistling another tired song."*

*"Engines hum and bitter dreams grow
a heart locked in a Gran Torino
it beats a lonely rhythm all night."*

*"Realign all the stars above my
head."*

*"I drink instead on my own Oh!
how I've known
the battle scars and worn out beds.
[…]"*

*"May I be so bold and stay
I need someone to hold
[…]"*

*"Engines hum and better dreams
grow."*

Match themes from the box with the song lyrics and explain your decisions. Add more themes if you can.

self-acceptance – self-judgment – self-reflection – old age – loneliness – nostalgia – haunting memories – the need to belong – affection – exhaustion – hope – change – regrets – endurance – tranquility

5. Conclusion: Sense of belonging

Summarize the significance of the contents of Walt's will. Assess what they reveal about Walt's sense of belonging, and analyze the effect it has on Thao's sense of belonging.

Walt's sense of belonging	Thao's sense of belonging

The Ambiguity of Belonging: Walt's development

"Dad's still living in the 50s." (Walt's son Steve)

a. *Walt Kowalski is a fossil, out of place in a world where everything (objects, people, values) has changed or deteriorated. Describe Walt's present life (at the beginning of the movie) in contrast to his past life.*

	Walt's past life	**Walt's present life (beginning of the movie)**
Historical background	Detroit in the 1950s: peak population of 1.8 million; well-paid jobs in the automobile industry	Detroit in the 21st century: decline of the auto industry, unemployment, dramatic drop in population, entire neighborhoods are abandoned
His house/his neighbourhood/ his community	well-maintained house in a safe neighborhood where mostly white middle-class people/automobile workers lived; he went to church because it was important to his wife	
His job	worked all of his life for the Ford Motor Company assembling cars; put the steering column on his own Gran Torino	
His family	was married to the best wife he could imagine, had two sons, never had a close relationship with his sons	
His doctor	Dr. Feldman used to be his (experienced, male, white) doctor.	
War/violence/ crime	• fought as a soldier in Korea • won a Silver Medal for his service • killed people, even a teenager • lost many friends in the battle • learned to rely on himself and to defend himself.	

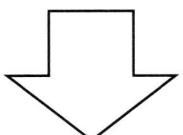

Remaining moments of warmth and belonging in Walt's present life:
- *sitting on his porch with his dog, drinking beer, admiring his Gran Torino in the driveway*
-
-
-

b. *Evaluate your findings and interpret Walt's ambiguity of belonging. Describe the ambivalence he experiences and comment on the emotional consequences it has on Walt. You can also refer to these quotes:*

[Sue translating what the Hmong shaman says about Walt:]
He says the way you live, your food has no flavor. You're wearied by your life.
You made a mistake. And your past life is like a mistake what you did. You are not satisfied with.
He says, you have no happiness in your life. It's like you are not at peace.

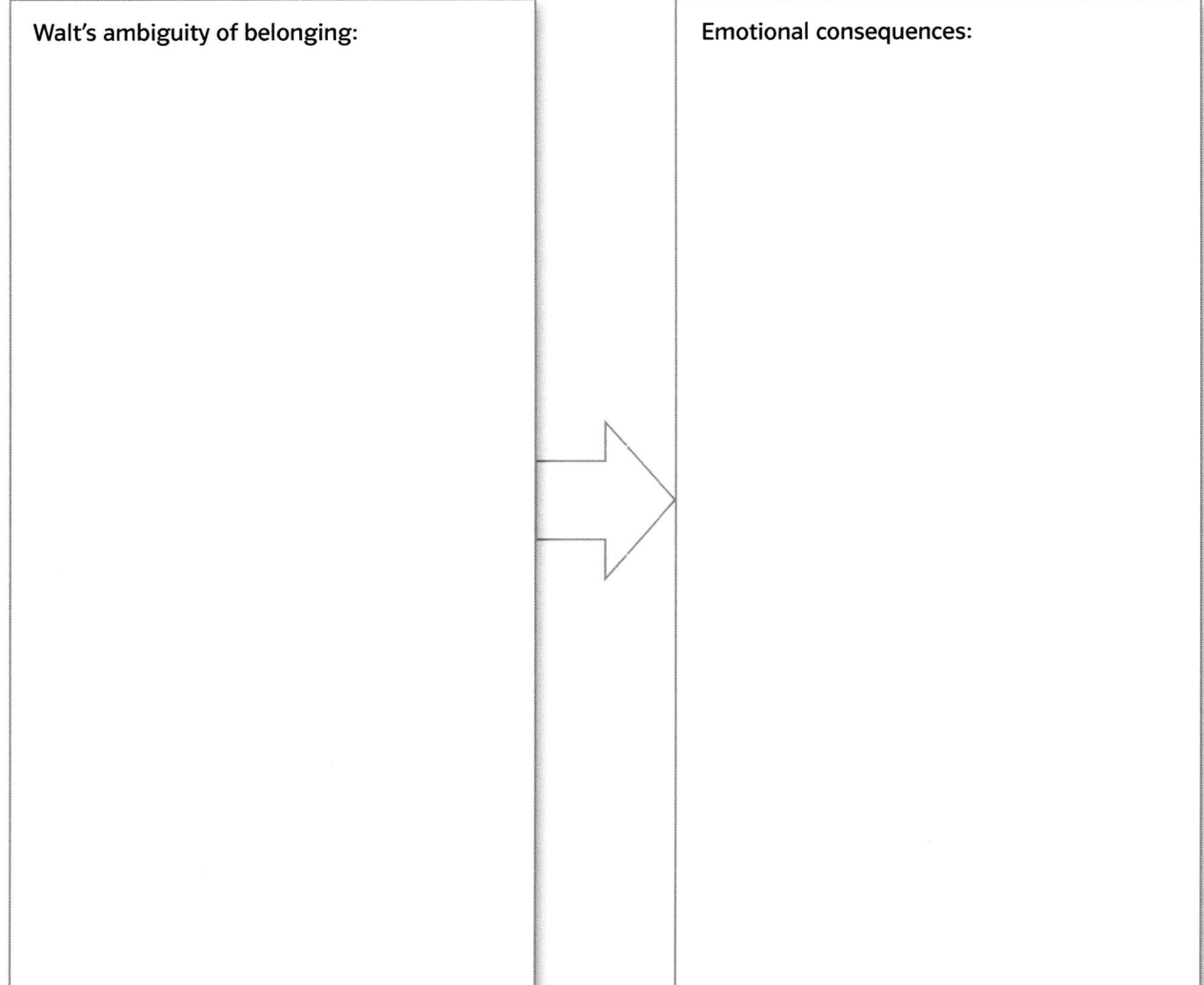

Walt's ambiguity of belonging:

Emotional consequences:

The Ambiguity of Belonging: Thao's development

> "He just doesn't know which direction to go in." (Sue)

1. Thao's lack of direction

Read through the list of possible reasons for Thao's lack of orientation at the beginning of the movie.
With your partner discuss their significance and agree on the three most important ones.

- He doesn't have a father or a male role model in his family.
- He doesn't fit into his traditional Hmong family, and yet he is seen as a suitable (future) man of the house.
- He is a boy with qualities that are commonly seen as female; he is rather submissive and introverted and lets Sue order him around. He does "women's work" in the kitchen and the yard. His name is commonly used as a girl's name.
- He doesn't go to school, has no job and no idea about what to do with his life.
- He's different from other young Hmong men in the movie (reads books, helps the old lady next door, etc.).
- He doesn't seem to have any friends (e.g. at the party he is all by himself), the only people interested in him are the Hmong gangbangers.

2. Thao's ambiguity of belonging: Boy or men? Hmong or American?

a. *Analyze Thao's outer appearance, his behaviour and how other people treat him in the course of the movie.*
What aspects make him appear like a boy or a young man, like a Hmong or like an American?

Thao, the boy	Thao, the young man

The Hmong Thao	The American Thao

b. *Summarize your findings and describe Thao's development. Examine if or how Thao finally reaches some sense of belonging.*

Klausur (mit Hörsehverstehen): Gran Torino

I Comprehension (DVD 00:59:33 – 01:04:42)

1. Sentence completion   (2 VP)

Complete the sentences in a meaningful way.

Walt calls his son Mitch in order to …

_____

Walt lies to his son, because …

_____

2. Complete the table   (4 VP)

From the box choose the adjective that best describes the character's state of mind in the given situation and write it into the table. Each adjective can only be used once.

	Mitch is …	**Walt is …**
Beginning of the phone call,		
Right after the phone call,		

> thoughtful – furious – self-confident – confused – estranged – insecure –
> proud – superior – annoyed – surprised – excited

3. True or false   (4 VP)

Tick the correct statements. Correct the false ones.

	true	false
a. Walt asks Thao to turn on the fan to see if it is working.	☐	☐
b. Thao wants to know how much the tools are worth.	☐	☐
c. Walt says that it takes half a century to buy such an assortment of tools.	☐	☐
d. With the three objects Walt gives to Thao, many problems can be fixed.	☐	☐

II Analysis. Choose ONE of the following.   (10 VP)

1.

> Clint Eastwood's films "explore the possibilities of relationships that go beyond the everyday and explore moments of guilt, forgiveness, redemption, hope, and love."
> (David H. Calhoun)

Explain the quote, referring to the given film sequence and other scenes from the movie.

2. *Imagine Walt looked into the mirror in his bedroom after the phone call with his son and talked to himself. Write his monolog.*

III Composition. Choose ONE of the following.   (10 VP)

1.

> "As a second-generation Hmong American, I felt I was living in a trapped world, spilling back and forth between two different cultures. In the mornings, I went to school and became "American." I spoke English, ate hamburgers for lunch, and hung out with friends, all the while pretending I came from the same sort of family background as my American friends did. In the afternoon, I returned home to be "Hmong." … Being born in America, I will never fully understand the Hmong culture, not the way my parents and the other elders do…. Because of this, I knew I could never be the person my parents wanted me to be. … I found myself stuck."
> (Quoted from: The Asian American Cultural Alienation Scale: Development, Factor Analysis …) by Agnes Wing Yan Kwong)

Comment on the quote and relate it to Thao in the film Gran Torino.

2. *In his will, Walt leaves his Gran Torino to Thao and his house to the church.*
    Write Father Janovich's sermon for the following Sunday, in which he talks about the significance of these gifts.

Reading Comprehension	10 VP	
Analysis Content	10 VP	
Analysis Language	15 VP	
Composition Content	10 VP	
Composition Language	15 VP	
Gesamt	**60 VP**	

III Anhang: Lösungshinweise

I Hinführung zum Film

KV 3: Gran Torino: Movie trailer

1. Die Zuordung der Adjektive ist nicht eindeutig. Eigenschaften wie 'predictable' oder 'entertaining' können als negativ oder auch positiv gesehen werden.
   Gut möglich wäre aber:
   Positive: vigorous, humorous, insightful, entertaining, well-paced, thought-provoking, compelling, touching
   Neutral: realistic, earnest
   Negative: predictable, macho, gritty, clichéd, radical
2. Individuelle Lösungen.
3. Abweichende Lösungen möglich. Denkbar (= real im Film) ist:
   The most dominant conflict is between Walt and the Asian gang.
   Dominant conflict between Walt and the priest – relationship seems to improve
   Dominant conflict between Walt and his neighbors/Thao/Sue – relationship seems to improve
   Underlying/lesser conflicts: Walt and his family; Hispanic/Asian gangs; Sue+white boy/Black gang

KV 4: Gran Torino: Movie poster

1. and 2.:
- Stark contrast between dark and bright, black and white – apart from the golden letters and the shades of grey, the only colors in the picture.
- Bright front of Walt's body stands out against black background and dark shadow on Walt's body.
- Walt's legs, stomach, chest and the side of his face, which he is turning towards the viewer, are all illuminated as if lit up by a flashlight.
- The darkness, the fierce look on Walt's face and the rifle suggest evil, crime, violence, revenge, etc.
- Bright side of Walt's body and his calm appearance evoke positive associations like strength, prudence, protection, rescue, law and order, justice, control or even insight and revelation.
- Golden letters of the title form the most dominant horizontal line in the foreground.
- Stylized upright body of Walt Kowalski (from knee to head) constitutes the most prominent vertical line, filling about a third of the picture.
- If one extended the horizontal line (made by the worded title on the left of the poster) further to the right, one would have the perfect shape of a cross.
3. Possible **genres**: thriller, action, Western, drama. Possible **plot**: escalating conflict between gangs or neighbors. Possible **themes**: violence, crime, punishment, revenge, isolation, good/evil, law and order.

KV 5: Gran Torino: Speed viewing

1. Individuelle Antworten.
2. Mögliche Antworten: courage, family, fear, freedom, friendship, heroes, love and hate, peer pressure, prejudice, pride, religion, revenge, security/safety, war and peace.
3.

"American" moment	→	stands for…
American flag (omnipresent in the movie!)	…	**freedom**, greatness, unity
Weapons: gun, rifle, shootout	…	the right to bear arms; **self-defense**
The priest	…	the importance of **religion**
White truck	…	mobility; **self-reliance**
Drinking beer from cans	…	convenience, manliness
House with front porch and yard	…	American dream, **family**

4. *Good and Evil, The Savior, The Hero of the Neighborhood, Revenge, The Clash, The Hero.*

KV 6 und 7: Historical background

2. Both texts deal with the US involvement in Asia during the Cold War. In the Korean War the US supported the southern part of the divided country to contain communism. In Vietnam the US sent troops and recruited Hmong soldiers to help them fight a hopeless guerilla battle against the Viet Kong.

KV 8: Detroit – a two-sided city

1. The bathtub metaphor tries to illustrate that recent investments have little effect on the poor.
   line(s) 20–22   ✐ "It does little (…) the city's residents."

2. In the past 15 years Detroit has changed because many families fled to the suburbs.
   line(s) 26–27   ✐ "Half of its (…) in the suburbs."

3. Midtown and Corktown are neighbourhoods where you can only live if you have a decent income.
   line(s) 43–44   ✐ "The problem is (…) to live here."

EXTRA: Walt's neighborhood has changed. He seems to be the only survivor of a white middle class which moved away when they lost their jobs due to Detroit's economic crisis.

II   Working with the film: Modul A: Theme Club Project

KV A1: Theme Group: Prejudices and racism

1. **Getting started: Everyday racism**
a. – Speaker assumes that the boy was born in Korea, although many Asian Americans are born in the US and have never left the US.
   – Speaker presumes that the boy's first language is "Asian" or Korean, although the boy is American.
   – Speaker reveals his own ignorance, since he does not know which language is spoken in Korea.

b. – Prejudices and racism are often rooted in insecurity and fear.
   – Racial jokes are no longer acceptable in times of political correctness.

2. **Watching the movie: Walt Kowalski's racism**
   a. <u>Language</u>: numerous racial slurs ("swamp rats", "zipper head", "gooks", "eggroll", etc), vulgar remarks ("Get the shit out of your mouth"; "We used to stack fucks like you six feet high in Korea"), stereotypes about ethnic groups ("jungle people", "All you slopes are supposed to be good at math, right?"), overtly racist insults ("You people are nuts", "These Hmong broads are like badgers"), racist jokes ("A Mexican, a Jew and a coloured guy go into a bar…"); speaks in a very harsh tone, growls at people
   <u>Behavior/actions</u>: very rude: does not lend jumper cables to Thao, spits towards the Hmong grandmother, rejects Hmong presents, makes fun of Thao (count the birds in the tree).
   BUT: protects the Hmong family: chases away the gang, saves Sue in the black neighborhood, finds Thao a job, sacrifices himself to save Thao and Sue.

   b. Walt's (racist) development in the course of the movie

   Walt keeps his racist façade (racist language) until the end, but his behaviour shows that his attitude has changed towards more openness, empathy and tolerance. In the beginning he sees all Asians as "gooks" and "barbarians", but through his relationship to Sue and Thao he learns to see people as individuals whose moral standing and "worth" does not depend on their ethnicity. Walt understands that people's "strange" behavior is often an expression of their cultural traditions and conventions.

c. Walt's racist behaviour shouldn't be excused, but it becomes clear that Walt is "a good man", as Sue puts it. He lives according to honorable moral principles and beliefs, for instance: "Everybody has the right to live in peace and to be left alone"; "You must help and protect the weak and the helpless (especially women)"; "You must work hard", "Never complain and rely on yourself", "You must stick to your country's traditions and values". This conservatism connects him with Thao and Sue's traditional family.

3. Watching closely: Roots of racism

a.

Walt's preconceptions about the Hmong	Sue's reactions
Asian girls are smart.	Sue doesn't respond. But in the course of the conversation She proves that she is quick-witted, funny and smart.
The "Humong" shouldn't mix with whites.	Sue corrects him and exposes his ignorance for the first time.
Walt thinks that Hmong is a country.	Sue uses irony to uncover his ignorance ("You're so enlightened, you know that?"): Hmong is not a place but a people that comes from three Asian countries.
Walt assumes the Hmong came to the US for no good reason.	Sue gives him a short history lesson. The Hmong fought for the US in Vietnam. For this, they were persecuted politically.
He imagines them to be "jungle people".	Sue corrects Walt once again: The Hmong are *hill* people. He makes fun of his stereotypical view.
"You think the cold would keep all the idiots out."	Sue doesn't take this remark as an insult but as a joke, which makes her appear self-confident and superior.
Walt thinks that Thao is stupid.	Sue contradicts him, saying Thao is smart but lacks direction.

b. Walt's lack of knowledge makes him see the Hmong as savage "jungle people" and "barbarians", who have invaded his country and neighborhood. Ignorance can easily lead to prejudice, which seems to bridge gaps in knowledge. Lack of knowledge can result in uncertainty and fear of the unknown. Other reasons: his horrifying experience in Korea, brainwashing him to see all Asians as enemies; his life as a white minority in an Asian-American neighborhood; his general mistrust (he can't trust his own family).

c. In the first shot, through the windshield, Sue appears to be small next to Walt, who tells her off for behaving so irresponsibly. But then in all subsequent shots, a **camera angle** is chosen which shows Sue ➔ **on an eye-to-eye level** with Walt. There is a striking cinematic symmetry during the dialogue: the camera jumps evenly from Walt to Sue, showing them in identical **field sizes** for about the same length of time.

4. Exploring further: Eastwood accused of racism

- Accusations against Eastwood: the Hmong actors were discriminated against on set. They were forced to represent their culture and their people in an inaccurate way. The film sheds a negative light on the Hmong: The overtly racist language is very offensive. Asians are represented in a stereotypical way.

- Counter-arguments: the racist language is part of a realistic picture of the US. Making or laughing about racist jokes does not turn a person into a racist. The movie gave the Hmong minority in the US their first chance to be seen and heard by a broad audience.

KV A2: Theme Group: Masculinity

1. **Getting started: The man card**

   Additional tasks 'for a 'man card'': smoking cigars, playing poker, winning a fist fight against someone, winning a (sports) competition, dating the most beautiful girls, traveling to a foreign country alone, getting a tattoo or a piercing, programing a computer, owning a car

   Mögliche Lösungen: Qualities of 'real' men: honesty, loyalty, reliability, tolerance, respect, taking responsibility for your actions, etc.
   EXTRA: Individuelle Lösungen

2. **Watching closely: Walt's masculinity**

   a.

Actions/Deeds	Language	Symbols (actual objects)
shows little emotion and is disciplined; protects his property, fixes things; helps/defends others; uses firearms; drinks beer and whiskey and goes to the local pub; drives a pick-up truck; worked for Ford, assembled his own car; got married, has two sons; hides his illness, never complains; relies on himself, doesn't ask for help; went to war.	growls; ironical remarks; ("You've just painted your nails"); vulgar language; ("Come on, get the shit out of your mouth"); overtly racist language; ("zipper head"); commanding tone; ("Bullshit. This is a bar. You have a drink.")	rifle; gun; white truck; muscle car/Gran Torino; garage; tools; beer/whiskey; zippo lighter; war memorabilia (Silver Medal); American flag; his house and yards.

   b. individuelle Lösungen

3. **Watching closely: Manning up Thao**

   a.

	In the backyard	At the construction site
Content: The setting and Thao's actions (what image does this give him?)	Thao is working in Walt's yard/polishing Walt's car/gardening without making any money/doesn't have any idea what to do with his life. Spreading mulch in a small backyard corresponds to Thao's lack of perspective, experience and ambition.	Thao is having an informal job interview/ following Walt/trying to speak to Kennedy as Walt told him to do. The construction site stands for manliness, strength, future prospects, ambition, progress etc.
Language: How Thao speaks and reacts	His language mirrors his insecurity: he asks many questions, uses 'maybe', takes Walt's teasing remark seriously ("Yeah you're right, nobody would ever hire me.").	His body language still shows insecurity, but he has learned how men talk. He answers Kennedy's questions in a "manly way": polite but lying and swearing to look tough.
Camera angle and field size	Camera switches from over-the-shoulder shots, which look down on Thao squatting in the vegetable bed, to eyelevel medium shots of Thao looking up to Walt whose full body is shown.	Almost exclusively eye-level shots of Thao. Mostly medium, some close-up shots of Thao, who moves to the foreground during the interview with Kennedy so that he appears to be as tall as the super.
Conclusion	In the first scene, the camera emphasizes Walt's superiority as mentor or father figure and Thao's insecurity, weakness and submissiveness. In the second scene, Walt continues to lead and instruct Thao, whose appearance still lacks self-confidence (rocking movements, looking down on the floor). Yet during the interview the camera makes Thao appear more grown-up and mature.	

   b. Abweichende Lösungen. In the beginning Walt acts like a teacher and trainer. By the end he has become a friend and a substitute father.

4. **Exploring further: Femininity in Gran Torino**

Individuelle Lösungen.

Although Sue becomes a helpless victim of the Hmong gang's violence and brutality, she is a strong character: she gives Thao orders, she is not afraid of Walt and she breaks the ice between the neighbors, she is extremely quick-witted; in verbal exchanges she beats the Hmong gang, the black gang and even Walt.

KV A3: Theme Group: Gran Torino

1. **Getting started: The significance of cars**
   a. Individuelle Lösungen
   b. Description: muscle car, sports car, elegant silhouette/shape/form, not a luxury car.
      (Stereo-)typical driver: male, white, middle-class, maybe patriotic, emphasizes his masculinity, treasures his car, the car serves as a status symbol, etc.

2. **Watching the movie: the role of (Walt's) Gran Torino**
   a. and b.

Action	Significance for Walt or Thao	Function of the scene
During the funeral reception Walt discovers Ashley sneaking a cigarette in his garage. She seems to have uncovered the Gran Torino.	Represents something old and precious that Walt seems to be hiding from his family. Ashley is interested in the material value of the vintage car, she knows little of her grandfather's past and what the car means to him.	Viewer is introduced to the Gran Torino as Walt's hidden treasure, a remnant of his past. The ending is foreshadowed: Ashley expects to inherit the car, but Walt leaves it to Thao, to whom he feels closer than to his own family.
The Hmong gang admires the Gran Torino when they see it outside. Thao should steal it (initiation).	By stealing the Gran Torino Thao is supposed to prove his courage, his manliness and his desire to belong to the gang.	The car is shown as an object of envy, since even the Hmong gang members know about its technical features and its special value.
Thao tries to steal the Gran Torino at night and is almost shot by Walt.	Walt is prepared to shoot trespassers who try and steal his "treasure".	Ironically it is Thao's crime that makes them friends. Walt learns that Thao is not a thief who needs to be punished, but a victim of the Hmong gang.
Walt works lovingly on the Gran Torino in his drive.	see: "Role/significance of the Gran Torino", in 3, p. 97.	
Thao washes the Gran Torino in the backyard. Walt promises to lend Thao the car for his date with Youa.	It is a sign of confidence and affection that Walt lets Thao wash his car. As Sue says: "Kind of ironic. Toad washing the car that he tried to steal from you."	In the previous scene it is Walt who polishes the Gran Torino, now it is Thao. This foreshadows the ending, when Thao – not Ashley – inherits the car from Walt.
Thao and Sue drive the Gran Torino to the shoot-out.	It seems natural that Thao drives the Gran Torino.	It's the first time we see Thao drive the Gran Torino, but we barely notice it in the tumult following Walt's death.
After Walt's death Thao takes the Gran Torino for a run on Lake Shore Road.	see: "Role/significance of the Gran Torino", in 3, p. 97.	

3. **Watching closely: looking after the Gran Torino**

a.

	Scene 1: Walt and his Gran Torino	Scene 2: Thao inheriting Walt's legacy
Emotions	Walt is proud of his car; he seems to be satisfied with what he has achieved in life, and has an affectionate relationship to his car, treating it almost like a (female) human being: "Ain't she sweet?"	Thao is sad about Walt's death; still he seems to feel good behind the wheel of the Gran Torino, taking Walt's place. He appears relieved and free to choose his own way without being pressured.
Camera (angle and field size)	Camera is positioned at a "headlight" level, it follows Walt walking around the car, polishing the front. Walt is shown from a low angle as he is bending down to his car. The next shots switch back and forth from Walt's perspective (high angle over-the-shoulder shots looking at the car) to the Gran Torino's perspective (low angle shots, looking up to Walt) as if they are having a conversation.	First shot: medium shot at eye-level of Thao through the windshield; the camera zooms in to a close up. Second shot: Long shot at eye-level; the camera is panning from right to left to follow the Gran Torino driving along the lake shore and until it disappears in the distance. The camera freezes the picture for the closing credits.
Colors/ lighting	Evening sun, warm light, long shadows, soft colors create an emotional, almost romantic atmosphere. At the end of the scene it has become dark and Walt switches on the porch light.	From the dark corner of the notary's room the shot dissolves into daylight with Thao driving the Gran Torino. The second shot opens up to sunshine, endless blue water and blue sky. The white lighthouse at the horizon appears like a symbol of orientation and hope.
Music (theme song 'Gran Torino', sung by Clint Eastwood)	Instrumental version of the soft, slow, melancholy and soothing theme song, underlines the sentimentality of the scene.	Instrumental introduction of the theme song starts when Thao learns that he has inherited the Gran Torino. The vocal part begins with the dissolve into the lake drive scene. Walt seems to be present with Thao in the car through his remarkable voice. The soft, sad but also comforting music matches Thao's state of mind.
Role/ significance of the Gran Torino	Walt's seems to feel a personal bond to his car. The Gran Torino is a part of Walt, since he assembled it himself and it is one of the few things that remain from his past.	The car makes Thao more mature, more manly and more American. It gives him social status. It also makes him more independent from his family and stands for the new mobility and freedom he now has. It shows that he has accepted Walt's legacy, his "old-school" values and principles of hard work, self-reliance, loyalty and honesty. Walt is "present" through his singing voice.

4. Movies with cars that are like human beings: *Herbie, Cars*. Movies with cars that mirror their owners' personalities: VW Bus in *Little Miss Sunshine*, James Bond cars. Movies with cars that provide action and entertainment: *The Italian Job*; *The Blues Brothers*.

KV A4: Theme Group: Violence

1. **Getting started: Violence starts with thoughts**
   a. Individuelle Lösungen
   b.

6. Committing
murder/suicide

5. Armed assault

4. Pushing physically, standing in sb's way

3. Attacking verbally, intimidating, threatening behavior

2. Ignoring and excluding sb, spreading rumours

1. Teasing/ridiculing sb's appearance or behavior

2. **Watching the movie: Escalating violence**
   a.

Characters involved	Violent behavior	Your comment
Thao, Hmong gang	Gang members verbally harass Thao, putting pressure on him to join their gang.	Already the third level of violence; Thao has no chance against the group.
Thao, Walt	Thao breaks into Walt's garage to steal the car as an initiation rite; runs away from the gang.	Thao is forced to commit a crime and to involve Walt in the conflict.
Thao, his family, Hmong gang, Walt	The Hmong gang tries to force Thao to get into their car. The conflict escalates into a fight between Thao's family and the gang. Walt gets involved as the gang trespasses on his property. He ends the fight by threatening them with a rifle.	Walt brings the conflict to a higher level by using a weapon.
Thao, the Hmong gang	The Hmong gang attack Thao going home from work. They brutally burn the helpless boy's cheek with a cigarette as if to mark him as coward.	For the first time someone gets hurt. The cigarette serves as weapon in a one-against-five situation.
Walt, Smokie	Walt waits until one gang member is on his own to beat him up, taking revenge for Thao's burns. He threatens the gang, trying to get them to leave Thao alone.	Walt tries to end the conflict but paradoxically does the contrary: his violent attack only contributes to a further escalation.
Hmong gang, the van Lors	The Hmong gang terrorizes Thao and Sue's family with a drive-by shooting, using automatic weapons. They brutally rape and beat up Sue.	The gang is cold-blooded, ruthless and stops at nothing. Only by chance is nobody seriously hurt in the shooting.
Walt, the Hmong gang	Walt shows up at the gang's house and pretends to seek vengeance. All the Hmong gangsters shoot him and are arrested for murder.	Walt breaks the spiral of violence by sacrificing himself. For the first time he trusts in the police and the rule of state law to ensure justice.

   b. Walt could have asked the priest to act as a mediator. He could have tried to talk to the gang to find a diplomatic solution. He could have called the police.

3. Watching closely: Walt as a hero of violence

a.

Action	Atmosphere	Film techniques (camera movements, lighting, sounds/music)
The Hmong gang show up	Dark, tense, gloomy	Dark setting, only the Hmong gang's white car is lit, the music stops when the car stops. The car is dark inside; it is unclear how many people are inside. The camera seems to take Sue and Thao's point of view, before Smokie invades their home.
Gang members violently ...	Turbulent, panicky, frightening, out of control	As soon as Smokie forces Thao to go with him, the camera starts moving faster and faster; shots get shorter, close-up shots of legs and feet make the scene even more dramatic and underline that the situation has gotten out of control. People are screaming.
Walt shows up and	Still threatening and tense, but no longer chaotic and frantic	The screaming dies down as soon as we hear Walt's calm, dark voice and see him pointing his rifle at the intruders in a composed way. The camera is static again. Dramatic, drumming music starts. Characters' faces are only partially lit. In close-up shots, Walt's bright face seems to glow in the dark. The music turns into a single sound when the car drives away.

a. Other techniques: more music, slow motion, (extreme) close-up shots of faces, etc.
b. Individuelle Lösungen. Alle Aussagen können belegt oder angefochten werden.

4. Exploring further: Gran Torino as a mirror of American culture

Belief in:

- self-defense and self-reliance;
- the right to carry and use arms;
- individual freedom (instead of government control);
- individualism and privacy;
- one's country and its traditions (patriotism);
- hard work and success.

KV A5 Theme group: Religion

1. Getting started: Existential questions and religious symbols

a. Christian cross (crucifix): universal symbol of Christian faith, stands for both suffering and defeat but also triumph and salvation; represents the crucifixion of Jesus Christ; symbolizes atonement for our sins and God's love, as God sacrificed his only son.
Fire/light: indicates the presence of God; is a symbol of the Holy Spirit; in the contrast between good and evil, light stands for the good and the divine.

b. Existential question in religions: "What comes after death?", "What is good? What is evil?", "How can we find forgiveness?", "Why does an almighty God allow suffering?", "Should humans be allowed to decide over life and death (e.g. abortion, euthanasia, suicide, death penalty)?"

2. Watching the movie: References to Christian faith

a.

Phrase of film	Elements of Christianity
Beginning Ending	• Funeral, eulogy: "life and death", funeral service • Priest: Father Janovich (the Good Shepherd) looking after Walt (or trying to), who is one of the "sheep from his flock"); asking him to go to confession • 5th commandment: "Honor your father and mother." –> Walt's sons and grandchildren do not honor or respect Walt. • Old Testament: "an eye for an eye" mentality that leads to the escalation of the conflict • New Testament: "Love your neighbour as yourself" • Walt's official confession at church • Walt's personal confession to Thao, when Thao is locked in the basement • Walt's last words "Me I've got a light" and his Christ-like death • Walt lives on in Thao, who has adopted Walt's values and has inherited his Gran Torino → Walt/Clint Eastwood's voice in the theme song at the very end.

b. <u>Symbolism of light</u>: Walt has had his zippo lighter on him for over 50 years. He provokes the Hmong gang to execute him by drawing this lighter from his pocket like a gun. Light stands for the presence of God and the good in Walt (Sue: "But you're a good man, Wally").

<u>Symbolism of the Christian cross (crucifix)</u>: Walt's death reminds the viewer of Christ's passion, since Walt sacrifices his own life to save Thao and Sue, and also because he is lying on the ground in a cross-shaped position, blood running from his hands. The movie poster also hints at the shape of a cross/crucifix.

3. Watching closely: Walt's death

a.

	Description	Effect
Colors and lighting	Night, darkness, light from houses; Walt's body melts into the darkness because of his dark clothing; he steps into the light (of a street lamp?) when he approaches the house so that his right side is illuminated; hitting the ground, his hand with the lighter opens up and is brightly illuminated.	Darkness creates a gloomy atmosphere and increases the tension; Walt being in the dark foreshadows his death; however the light on his face and his body indicate that his secret, dark plan will bring peace and hope; the spotlight on the lighter in his hand reveals that he is unarmed and dies innocently.
Camera (angles, movements, field size) and special effects	Camera zooms in on Walt, follows every hand gesture; field size shrinks from mostly full and long shots to medium and close up shots; special effect: slow motion/sound when Walt is falling down to the ground, music starts; in the final crane shot the camera moves across Walt's body and rises into the air (like an angel or as if his "light"/soul is leaving his body), showing his cross-shaped position.	The focus is on Walt, the tension increases, the viewer waits for Walt to pull his gun; the brutal execution shocks the viewer; but afterwards the viewer finds release and peace through the slow motion, the music and the calmly moving camera.

b. Walt is partly responsible for the Hmong gang's attack on Sue, since he contributed to the escalation of the conflict. Walt sacrifices himself to put an end to the downward spiral of violence. He killed a teenage boy in Korea, although the boy had surrendered. With his own death, Walt pays for this sin by saving the life of an Asian boy (Thao), who is probably about the same age as the Korean boy had been.

c. Individuelle Lösungen.

4. **Exploring further: Invisible religion**
   Matrix and other science fiction movies: What is the meaning of our existence? Who is our Creator?
   Traditional westerns and action films (e.g. older James Bond movies): What is good and what is evil?
   Romance and comedy: comfort and hope for a happy ending in a world full of misfortunes and suffering.

KV A1.L: Excel in language: Prejudices and racism (Lösungen auch im Schülerarbeitsheft)

1. 1. racism 2. racist (noun) 3. racist (adjective) 4. racial 5. race relations 6. race riot 7. racial profiling
2. a. – c. against (c: „about" geht auch); d. + e. to

KV A2.L: Excel in language: Masculinity (Lösungen auch im Schülerarbeitsheft)

1. Adjectives commonly associated with <u>masculinity</u>: ambitious, aggressive, rebellious, self-confident, forceful, protective, individualistic, non-emotional, tough-skinned, competitive, independent, athletic, dominant, active (neu).
   Adjectives commonly associated with <u>femininity</u>: dependent, emotional, accepting, submissive, graceful, flirtatious, nurturing, self-critical, passive, sensitive, understanding, tender, vulnerable, (neu) supportive
2. to rise to a challenge; to offer sb protection/safety/one's strength; to take revenge on sb; to provide safety to sb/sb protection/the father role for sb; to adopt the father role for sb; to demonstrate one's strength; to suppress one's emotions; to use violence/one's strength against sb

KV A3.L: Excel in language: Gran Torino (Lösungen auch im Schülerarbeitsheft)

1. 1. Oldtimer 2. ein fantastisches/wunderschönes/glänzendes Auto 3. in perfektem Zustand sein 4. in ein Auto einsteigen 5. die Türe zuschlagen 6. in einem Auto davonfahren 7. die Reifen quietschen lassen
   8. ein Fahrzeug fährt an einer Stelle/einem Ort vor 9. ein Starthilfekabel an eine leere Batterie klemmen
   10. + 11. Eigene Antworten.
2. 1. *Do you promise to drive carefully?* – To control a vehicle (as a driver) well. 2. *Stop driving yourself so hard.* – To make someone work or try very hard. 3. *She drove him to the airport.* – To take someone to a place in a vehicle. 4. *You're driving me up the wall.* – To make someone extremely angry. 5. *They were driven out of their village.* – To force someone to leave a place.
3. a. Road, Street, Boulevard (in an address) b. hard drive (*Laufwerk in einem PC*) c. the desire to be successful and good at everything (*Tatendrang/Schwung*) d. *Drang, Triebe*, instinct e.g. sex(ual) drive

KV A4.L: Excel in language: Violence: Individuelle Lösungen

KV A5.L: Excel in language: Religion (Lösungen auch im Schülerarbeitsheft)

1. zur Beichte gehen 2. jdm/einem Pfarrer seine Sünden beichten 3. seine Schuld zugeben 4. etwas wiedergutmachen 5. seine Last/Sünden zurücklassen 6. jdn von seinen Sünden freisprechen 7. Erlösung finden 8. Er würde sich im Grab rumdrehen, wenn er das sehen könnte. 9. das Vaterunser 10. „Im Namen des Vaters, des Sohnes und des Heiligen Geistes" 11. vom Leben und dem Tod predigen 12. Gottesdienst.
More expressions: to pray for sb/sth, to go to church, to believe in God, to be religious/pious, resurrection

II. Working with the film: Modul B: The Ambiguity of Belonging

KV B1 und B2: Individuelle Lösungen

KV B3: The Ambiguity of Belonging: Quotes

Zusatzfrage: Different kinds of belonging: Belonging to yourself in the sense of self-acceptance, belonging to another person in a relationship, belonging to a group (e.g. family), belonging to a community.

KV B4: The Ambiguity of Belonging: Ethnic minorities

1. Individuelle Lösungen
2. a. **The man's immediate assumptions:** She is not American, since she looks Asian. She is not proficient in English. She eats Asian food. **Facts:** She was born in the US; sees herself as American. She is a native speaker of English. Just because her grandmother was Korean doesn't mean she only eats Korean food.
   b. Prejudices and racist attitudes of white people against people of color/Asian-Americans.
3a. "Hyphenated" Americans (Latino-Americans, African-Americans, Asian-Americans) are seen as different, as not fully belonging to society because of their ethnicity. This often causes an ambiguity of belonging in them, a feeling of being caught between two cultures.
   b. Individuelle Lösungen

KV B5: The Ambiguity of Belonging: The Language of belonging (Lösungen auch im Schülerarbeitsheft)

1. Das Nicht-wissen-wo-man-hingehört, die Ambivalenz des Dazugehörens, die ambivalente Zugehörigkeit
2. The center or root of the word 'belonging' is 'longing', which is a synonym for 'want'.
   Adjectives: e.g. a deep, desperate, great, intense, overwhelming, passionate, terrible, wild, sudden, hopeless, nostalgic, physical, sexual … longing
   Collocations: be filled with …, be full of …, feel/have a longing to do sth; his longing for sth
3. **Ambiguity** ~ incertitude, vagueness, double meaning, uncertainty, doubtfulness, enigma, obscurity, unclearness. **Belonging** ~ kinship, affinity, attachment, loyalty, relationship, inclusion, acceptance, association. Odd ones out: transition, challenge
4. **to belong (somewhere)** *hingehören (an einen Ort)* – **to belong to sb** *jdm gehören* – **to belong to sth** *zu etw. dazugehören, Mitglied sein* – **to belong to sb/sth** *zu einer Gruppe dazugehören* – **to feel a sense of belonging/ to have a feeling of belonging** *eine Zugehörigkeitsgefühl haben/spüren* – **to join sth** *einem Verein/einem Club beitreten* – **to join sb for sth** *mit jemandem etwas zusammen machen* – **to identify with sth** *sich mit etwas identifizieren* – **to participate in sth** *bei etw. mitmachen/an etwas teilhaben* – **to take part in sth** *an etwas teilnehmen* – **to be/feel part of sth** *sich zugehörig/als Teil von etwas fühlen* – **to exclude sb from sth** *jdn von etw. ausschließen* – **to be/feel excluded from sth/sb** *sich von etw/jdm ausgeschlossen fühlen*
5. Individuelle Lösungen

KV B6: The Ambiguity of Belonging: Character development

1. Rote Linie (Zugehörigkeitsgefühl zu den **Söhnen**): von Beginn an auf niedrigem Niveau, im Verlaufe des Films weiter abfallend durch die beiden Telefonate und den Geburtstagsbesuch.
   Blaue Linie (Zugehörigkeitsgefühl zu **Thao**): Beginn bei 0, ab Walts Geburtstag immer steiler ansteigend bis zu „deep sense".
   Grüne Linie (Zugehörigkeitsgefühl zu **Father Janovich**): Beginn bei 0, ansteigend mit jedem Gespräch ab Treffen in der Bar, erreicht jedoch kein „deep sense".
2. Zugehörigkeitsgefühl zu **Sue**: Zu Beginn nicht ganz eindeutig, wie tief die Verbundenheit Thaos zu seiner Schwester ist. Erst durch drive-by shooting wird sein Zugehörigkeitsgefühl deutlich; auch gemeinsame Fahrt zum Tatort am Ende.

Zugehörigkeitsgefühl zu **seiner Familie**: Von Beginn an auf eher niedrigem Niveau, einziger Hinweis auf positive Entwicklung: Grillen mit der Mutter in Walts Garten, Mutter begleitet Thao und Sue bei Walts Beerdigung. Zugehörigkeitsgefühl zu **Walt**: Zu Beginn niedrig, jedoch von Anfang an Respekt, Bewunderung. Steiler Anstieg durch Walts „Ausbildung" und offene Gespräche.

KV B7: The Ambiguity of Belonging: Opening sequence

2a. ... because Dorothy Kowalski, Walt's wife, has died.

b. ... because he lives in the past and might not be able to cope with the changes in his neighborhood.

c. ... since he cannot rely on them.

d. ... a box of stuff from his military service in the Korean War.

e. ... because this had been Dorothy's wish.

f. ... because he knocks on the door during the post-service reception.

g. ... (she would like to inherit) his couch and his Gran Torino.

h. ... "swamp rats".

i. ... in order to have a child blessing ceremony.

3a.

	Walt	Thao
Description of their family	White, middle-class adults; conventional appearance; children show no respect (clothing, behavior, language); Dorothy's death does not affect them emotionally, they show no genuine sympathy for Walt but instead appear superficial/self-centered.	Traditional family and community (clothing, food); respectful behavior; everybody brings food, the community seems to come before the individual, patriarchal structure ("man of the house").
Religious traditions/ ceremonies	Behave disrespectfully in church; do not take the ceremony seriously; Walt accuses people of showing up at the reception just for the ham.	Emotional involvement and belief in the ceremony, great respect for the shaman.
Behavior/ actions: what Walt and Thao say and do	Disdainfully observes both his family and the priest in church; does not participate in the reception; has no meaningful conversations with anyone; is sarcastic towards his family, arranges things (chairs), leaves the house (to get the jumper cables from the garage).	Doesn't participate in the gathering, quietly does the dishes in the kitchen, leaves the house to ask for jumper cables.
How the others see them	Is a grumpy, bitter old man who lives in the past and is incapable of having a warm relationship	Is a weakling: a young man who is too submissive and compliant to take on the vacant role of the patriarch.
How they seem to feel	Estranged, misjudged, alone (self-imposed isolation); apparently self-confident and superior.	Excluded, alienated, self-conscious, ill at ease.
Similarities	Both feel they are not really part of their own family, they don't belong. They don't participate in the ceremony, barely communicate with others. They both busy themselves with chores and leave the house.	
Differences	Walt appears very self-confident and shows open contempt for his family, while Thao lacks self-confidence and is obedient and submissive towards others.	

b. Neither character feels part of their family. Walt's feeling of estrangement and loneliness seems to be even stronger – he acts aggressively, whereas Thao just retreats.

4. Individuelle Lösungen

5. Individuelle Zusammenfassung der Lösungen

KV B8: Ambiguity of belonging: The gangs

2. 1. The Mexican gang members offend Thao **by ridiculing him for his feminine looks**.
   2. After … persuade Thao to get in the car **by saying that he must be thankful for their help**.
   3. When the Hmong gang shows up at the van Lor's place we find out **what Spider's real name is**.

3a. **Repetition** of "come on"; use of **imperatives**: "come on", "roll with us", "chill with us", "let's go"; they call him "dude", "man", "dawg" **to emphasize their comradeship**. They stress the **family bond** that already exists: "We're coz, right?" (2X), "We're family", "a brother to Spider is a brother to me."
They **promise** him entertainment, protection, belongingness, self-confidence and strength, masculinity.

3b. At first Spider squats down and Smokie bends down so that they are at eye level with Thao. They keep poking Thao, first in a playful way, but then increasingly more persistently. They take away his trowel and make him get up. Finally Spider rumples up Thao's hair like a little child.

3c. **Camera techniques**:
Camera angle: first eye level, then low level shot. Extreme **low angle shot** when Thao is standing:
→ **Effect:** emphasizes Thao's **inferior position** and weakness.
Field size/Composition: Mostly **medium** shots. Thao sits between the two tall gangbangers or is surrounded by the four men. **Focus on Thao**, who is framed by the Hmong men's moving arms and hands:
→ **Effect:** Thao appears to be jammed or trapped between the gangbanger like a helpless animal.
Camera movements: Slightly **moving camera** as long as Thao is sitting, then following Thao and swaying while he is getting up: → **Effect:** slight movements correspond to Thao's tense and rigid position, **swaying movements** mirror Thao's insecurity and lack of determination.

4a. i) **Flying solo:** You don't like the gang members. You do not share their interests: you are into gardening and reading and not into driving around and looking for trouble. You cannot trust them: they put pressure on you and get you to do things you don't want to do. You want to go to school, not to jail. Sue would be against your joining the gang…
ii) **Rolling with the gang:** You could gain some self-confidence. You would always have someone to support and protect you. This would finally bring some excitement into your life. Spider is your cousin, so he is one of you. You could prove to your family that you are a man who deserves respect…

5. Individuelle Zusammenfassung.

KV B9: Ambiguity of belonging: Language

2a. Sentences: 2 and 3 are correct. Corrected sentences: 1. Martin says Walt should come more often because after three weeks Walt doesn't look like a human being any more. 4. Walt doesn't say anything about his next haircut (but is just bantering).

2b. 1. Trey pretends to be one of the gang members.
   2. One of the African-Americans sexually harasses Sue with words and gestures.
   3. The gang feels provoked and threatens Trey.
   4. Sue is not intimidated, bravely defends herself.
   5. The gang doesn't know how to deal with Sue and becomes physically aggressive.
   6. The gang ridicules Walt because of his age.
   7. The gang acts in a defensive way.
   ~~Trey courageously tries to protect Sue.~~

3a.

	scene 1 **Walt and Martin**	scene 2 **The African-American gang members**
Similarities in the outer appearance	Same age, height, both European ancestors (Polish/Italian), blue-collar workers, white middle-class, conventional short-sleeved shirts, upright posture	About the same age; same ethnicity, similar dress code: sleeveless top, loose-fit pants, sneakers, short hair, tattoos, piercings, necklaces. They swing their arms, sway to and fro.
language used to show belongingness	Rough bantering, (racial) slurs like "you hard-nosed Pollack son of a bitch", "prick", "dipshit"; "are you half Jew?"	The f-word in all variations: "Shut the fuck up", "What the fuck..", "your motherfucking face". Discriminating language against women: "little tight ass", "bitch", "keep her on a leash"
"code" reveals … about the relationships	They show they share/have things in common/think alike. The bantering and (racist) insults are signs of hidden manly intimacy (since friendly or tender remarks would be seen as feminine).	All gang members follow rules about how to dress/talk. Trey looks ridiculous when he tries to copy the gang's style with his baseball cap and language. He shows that he is NOT part of the gang by using the words "bro" and "dawg", which the gang never use.

3b. Individuelle Lösungen

4. + 5. Individuelle Lösungen

KV B10: Ambiguity of belonging: Walt's birthday

2. 1. *What does Walt's horoscope say?*
    i) He has to make a choice between two life paths. ii) He gets second chances. iii) Extraordinary events culminate in what appears to be an anti-climax. iv) It gives him his lucky numbers.
    2. *Why does Walt get so angry …?*
    i) Their presents imply that he is a frail old man. ii) They want to put him into an old people's home, probably because they want to have his house.
    3. *How does Sue persuade Walt to come over..?*
    i) There is tons of food. ii) Walt can be her special guest. iii) They even have beer.
    4. *Rules of conduct Walt learns*
    i) Never touch a Hmong person on his/her head. ii) Don't look a Hmong person straight in the eye.
    iii) Hmong people smile when they feel embarrassed or insecure.
    5. *The shaman reads in Walt that:*
    i) people do not respect him and or even want to look at him. ii) the way he lives his food has no flavor. iii) he made a mistake in the past with which he is unhappy. iv) he has no happiness in his life/is not at peace.
    EXTRA: a. Andere Länder, andere Sitten!/Man muss mit den Wölfen heulen./Man soll sich den örtlichen Gepflogenheiten anpassen. Sue refers to proverbs like these with: "When in Hmong …", implying that you must respect/adopt customs of a culture when there. (*When in Rome, do as the Romans do.*")
3a. On the porch with Daisy: Medium level: Walt is alone but at ease with his cog. In his house: High level: Walt feels so misjudged and estranged that he gets very aggressive. At the Van Lors: High level at first: he feels out of place. Low level later, when he is sitting at the table surrounded by the Hmong women.

3b. • He sees that **Thao** is different from the other Hmong men in the neighbourhood. He shows respect for the Elder: He is polite and helpful.
   • He can tell that **Sue** really likes him and is really concerned about him when he coughs up blood.
   • He admires **Sue** for her quick-wittedness: He can banter with her like he can with his friends.
   • The **shaman** impresses him as he can "read" Walt's inner life better than his own sons or friends.
   • Even though he cannot fully understand the "strange" customs of **the Hmong**, he admires them because they respect conventions and traditions. The Hmong women give him a warm welcome at the table.
   • The Hmong also drink **beer**, so Walt has something in common with them. The **food** smells and tastes delicious (obviously better than his birthday cake and beef jerky). Walt can see that this is not the cuisine of "barbarians" who eat cats and dogs.

4. a. A symbol of physical reflection: Walt is an old man, who cannot hide his illness any more. Mostly a symbol of inner reflection and self-evaluation: he reflects on the experiences of his birthday, i.e. the disconcerting visit by Mitch and Karen and the values he shares with Sue and her family. A symbol of prophecy: Walt anticipates the friendship that will develop with Sue and Thao and the ending, where Walt leaves his treasure, the Gran Torino, to Thao instead of Ashley.
   b. Individuelle Lösungen, basierend auf den Beobachtungen in a.

5. Individuelle Zusammenfassung.

KV B11: Ambiguity of belonging: Thao's initiations

2. a. **Text 1:** Child blessing ceremony at the van Lor's. Thao is introduced in the context of his family. He will leave the house while everybody else is taking part in the ceremony.
   Text 2: On Walt's birthday at the Van Lor's barbeque, Walt has warmed up with the Hmong community before Sue takes him to the basement where the young people are hanging out and Walt meets Youa. Next day Thao's mother wants him to make amends for stealing the car by working for Walt for one week.
   Text 3: After working for Walt and the neighbors for a week, Thao has made up for his attempted theft. When Walt helps Thao fix a faucet, he realizes that the house is falling apart. He takes Thao to his garage to get some tools. The next time it is Walt that asks Thao for help – to carry the freezer up the stairs.
   b. **Second initiation:** Thao works for Walt and the neighbors for one week. He doesn't shy away from any job or weather. **Third initiation:** He must prove that he can talk and act like a man at the barber's shop. **Fourth initiation:** He goes to a job interview and and passes it.

3. a. **Do:** be polite; say hello; address a man with "Sir"; talk about your job, your car or your girlfriend/wife; **complain** about people who are not in the room; **use "manly" language** (including offensive racist slurs). **Don't:** insult or swear at the person you are talking to; **flatter people** (,,kiss ass"); **show your weaknesses**. Thao passes the test, but his body language still reveals insecurity and inexperience.
   b. Examples of racist language: "Perfect – a Polack and a Chink", "you crazy Italian prick", "you cheap bastard", "What are you doing? Jew a blind guy out of his money …?", "Who's the nip?"
   It's a common code they share, it shows that you belong since you know the unwritten rules, it creates a feeling of comradeship and intimacy between the people.

4. a. Individuelle Lösungen
   b. Individuelle Lösungen
   c. Walt has succeeded in turning Thao into a young man: He has a job and a girlfriend, he can fix things, has become more confident and less submissive. **Hmong notion of manliness:** a man should be "the man in the house". **American notion** (in Walt's eyes): A man is self-reliant: fixes things, defends himself and cares for his family, has a car that reflects him. We can only guess about how Thao's development changes his position in his family. He has gained respect by caring for them, fixing the house, buying a freezer, wanting to take revenge after the attack. Owning a car will certainly contribute to a higher standing.

5. Individuelle Zusammenfassung.

KV B12: Ambiguity of belonging: Walt's confessions and atonement

1. ***EXTRA:*** The present perfect is usually used to talk about a period in time that started in the past and continues to the present (or about something which has happened, and the user perceives it to have an effect on, or connection with, the present), e.g. "How long has it been since your last confession?" (the priest *wants him to confess now*). Or it is used to talk about unfinished actions or states, e.g. Walt's sins happened in the past, but Walt still feels the burden of these sins: "I've sinned", "It's (= it has) bothered me most of my life." (and the process is not over yet).
   Tense in Walt's confession: Simple past. Walt lists a number of finished actions in the past. The stress is on what he *did*, not on how this has burdened him since then.
2. Walt's confession to **Father Janovich**: He kissed a woman at a Christmas party behind Dorothy's back; he didn't pay taxes on the profit from a boat he once sold; he was never really close to his sons.
   Walt's confession to **Thao**: He killed a Korean boy that had surrendered. He shot him in his face.
   ***EXTRA:* Content:** Compared to the "murder" of the boy to which Walt confesses in the basement, the sins Walt confesses to the priest are negligible (since the poor relationship with his son is an inability rather than a sin). **Setting:** Walt only goes to church for Dorothy; it is not a place where he feels he belongs. His basement is a personal place, where he has hidden his sins in a trunk. Walt talks to Father Janovich in his function as a priest, not as a friend; Walt can be honest towards Thao, who has become a friend and almost a son.
3a. Individuelle Lösungen.
3b. If someone orders you to do something, you can blame the person for the consequences of your action; but if you make a decision alone, you carry the full responsibility for its consequences.
   Walt's mistakes: i) no close relationship to sons; ii) killing the Korean; iii) intensifying the gang conflict.
   How Walt makes up for them: *i) He is a father to Thao, who has no male role model. ii) He saves the life of a boy of the same age as the Korean. iii) He stops the gang from destroying Sue's and Thao's life.*
4a. "To be at peace" means to accept yourself and to have self-compassion, i.e. you don't judge yourself harshly for your personal failings but you are understanding and can forgive yourself.
4b. Individuelle Lösungen.
5. Individuelle Zusammenfassung.

KV B13: Ambiguity of belonging: Walt's will

2a. Thao must not: "**chop top**" the Gran Torino (chop topping is a pimping technique: pillars and windows are cut down in order to lower the car's roofline); **decorate it** with art (e.g. flames); put a **spoiler** on it.
2b. Walt's language from the notary's point of view: **offensive**; from Thao's point of view: **intimate**.
3a. *(Abweichende Lösungen möglich)* **Ranking at the beginning:** 1 notary 2 Mitch 3 Karen 4 Ashley 5 Steve 6 Thao. Notary has highest status, as he is independent and acts in an official position. Thao has the lowest status since he is not part of the family and appears out of place – he is the only one who has to remain standing. **Ranking at the end:** 1 notary 2 Thao 3 Steve 4 Mitch 5 Karen 6 Ashley. Thao's status is now above that of all family members, because he is the only person present who inherited something, although he expected nothing. Now the family members appear out of place at the notary, which lowers their status.
3b. At the beginning the ranking seems to depend on the character's ethnicity, social class, profession and family relation to Walt. In the end all these outer criteria do not count. It is Walt's friendship and affection that give Thao a high status.
3c. At the beginning Thao is standing in the back corner of the room in the dark, barely noticeable in the medium shot of the family; there are no close-up shots of him. After the will is read out, the camera switches from a medium shot of the room to a close-up shot of Thao. His face is lit so that we see first his surprise and then happiness. The theme song starts, and we remember his and Walt's friendship.
   EXTRA: Description: Gradual transition from Thao at the notary's to him sitting in the Gran Torino. For several seconds the two shots overlap. **Function:** It connects the two scenes and covers the time lapse. **Effect:** While the two shots are overlapping, the fading Thao appears to be sitting in the passenger seat, as if he was sitting next to Walt, giving the impression that Walt is present.

4a. Individuelle Lösungen.

4b. Thao has taken Walt's place or Walt is living on in Thao: Thao is driving Walt's car and taking care of his dog. Walt is present in the scene through his voice in the song.

4c. Ggf. gesamten Songtext einsetzen (aus Copyright-Gründen in diesem Heft nicht abgedruckt).

Self-acceptance: "do you belong in your skin, just wondering"; **self-reflection and self-judgment:** "Your story is nothing more than what you see or what you've done or will become."; **old age and exhaustion:** "another tired song", "bitter dreams grow", "a heart locked in a Gran Torino", "These streets are old"; **loneliness:** "it beats a lonely rhythm all night long", "I drink instead on my own", "a heart locked"; **nostalgia:** "They shine with the things I've known."; **haunting memories:** "How I've known the battle scars and worn out beds."; **need to belong and affection:** "so tenderly", "a tender breeze blows", "I need someone to hold"; **tranquillity:** "So tenderly", "gentle now", "a tender breeze blows", "whispering"; **change and hope:** "Gentle now a tender breeze blows", "Realign all the stars above my head", "better dreams grow"; **endurance:** "standing strong", "May I be so bold and stay"

5. Individuelle Zusammenfassung

KV B14: Ambiguity of belonging: Walt's development

1.

Walt's present life (beginning of the movie)

House/neighborhood/community: only white person still living in the only well-maintained house in a neighborhood where all white people have left and mostly Asian immigrants live; the church doesn't mean anything to him, he has no respect for the young, inexperienced priest

Job: retired, but keeps his house, yard and car in perfect condition; fixing things that don't need to be fixed

Family: has lost his beloved wife Dorothy, feels completely estranged from his two sons, their families and the lives they live, his only companion is his dog Daisy

Doctor: Feldman replaced by young female Asian, Dr. Chue, whose assistant can't pronounce his name.

War/violence/crime: burdened by war memories and feelings of guilt; defends his property and possessions, not relying on the police; answers violence with violence.

Remaining moments of warmth and belonging in Walt's present life:
- *sitting on his porch with his dog, drinking beer, admiring his vintage car in the driveway*
- *meeting his old friends at the bar, drinking, telling jokes*
- *getting a haircut and bantering with his old friend Martin, the barber*
- *talking to his friend Tim, the super at the construction site*
- *driving around in his white Ford truck*

---

b.

Walt's ambiguity of belonging:		**Emotional consequences:**
After his wife's death Walt is left alone in a world he can no longer identify with. The old have been replaced by the young, his white middle-class neighbors by Hmong immigrants, the new generation have forgotten about the past and do not share his old-school beliefs and values. Walt is still haunted by his horrible war experiences and burdened by his guilt.		Life without joy, lack of belongingness, feeling of being out of place, exhaustion, isolation, alienation, detachment, loneliness, dissatisfaction, regret, guilt, bitterness, unfriendliness, hostility.

KV B15: Ambiguity of belonging: Thao's development

1. Individuelle Lösungen.
2a. **Thao, the boy:** shy, obedient, submissive; does what his sister says. Doesn't have a job, hasn't learned any skills apart from doing the dishes and gardening. Helpless, cannot defend himself. Rather childlike features: small, skinny, not muscular. Insecure body language and facial expressions; doesn't have a girl-friend, doesn't know how to approach girls. People don't respect him (his own grandmother, gangs, Walt)
   Thao, the young man: Still withdrawn, but can get his own way (e.g. freezer scene). Has the necessary skills and manly demeanor to get a job at a construction site. Aggressive and ready to fight and even die to take vengeance after the Hmong gang's assault on the family. Has a job, a girl-friend and a car.
   The Hmong Thao: Part of Hmong community, although has no place either in family or in the gang. Hangs out with other Hmong teens; wears traditional clothing at Walt's funeral. Polite, respectful and helpful behavior is a result of a traditional Hmong upbringing. Probably speaks Hmong (Sue is bilingual).
   The American Thao: born in the US, native speaker; dresses like an American; adores the Gran Torino; admires Walt for his "old-school" American beliefs, Calvinistic work ethic, self-reliance, individualism and masculinity. Accepts Walt as an (American) role model: "manned up" by Walt, which also implies he is "Americanized". Final image of Thao: driving the Gran Torino alone (just with Daisy, not with Sue or Youa!); the setting mirrors American beliefs in mobility (the road) and opportunities (the endless blue sky and water).
2b. Individuelle Lösungen.

KV K: Klausur (mit Hörsehverstehen): Gran Torino

I Comprehension

1. Walt calls his son Mitch in order to **tell him about his illness/diagnosis.**
   Walt lies to his son because **he feels that he (his son) is bothered by his phone call.**
2. At the beginning of the phone call, Mitch is **annoyed** and Walt **insecure**
   Right after the phone call, Mitch is **thoughtful**; Walt **estranged**
3. a) **False:** Walt asks Thao to turn on the fan because it is very hot in the room.
   b) **False:** Thao wants to know why Walt has so many tools/what the tools are for.
   c) **True**
   d) **True**

II Analysis

1. Relationship between Walt and his son: the superficial conversation of the phone call reveals the **hollowness of a relationship** that lacks honesty, trust, real concern, compassion, understanding and respect, which leads to a feeling of alienation and isolation.
   Other scenes: 1. Mitch and Karen's visit on Walt's birthday. **Walt/Thao's relationship** breaks through the façade of both characters and reveals and deals with issues of real concern: Thao's lack of orientation and self-confidence and Walt's self-destructive guilt. **2.** Walt's confession to Thao in the basement.
2. Expresses his feeling of **estrangement and loneliness** and lack of trust. Asks himself why it isn't possible to break through the wall that stands between him and his sons. Looking at the wedding photo next to the mirror, he reflects on his loneliness after Dorothy's death. He can banter with his friends but has no one to talk to about his illness and the sins he fears he won't be able to repent before he dies. He thinks about his growing affection for Thao and Sue that has caused such a change in him.

III Composition

1. • Typical experience of a second generation immigrant caught between two cultures and living in constant ambiguity of belonging.
   • Thao and Sue are in similar situations, but Sue appears more Americanized and at ease than Thao.
   • Thao also feels he cannot be the person his family expects him to be: the man of the house.
   • As a result of this inner conflict Thao is disoriented, insecure and prone to peer pressure – a perfect victim for gangs, looking for people he can identify with and he feels he could belong to.
   • So Thao is not only caught between two cultures, but also between two genders (his feminine and his masculine side) and between two stages: boyhood and manhood.
   • Walt helps Thao out of the trap by manning him up and by imbuing him with American virtues.

2. Father Janovich expresses his personal affection and respect for Walt. He thanks Walt for his generous gift. He admits that Walt's decision to leave the house to the church was mostly influenced by Dorothy's wish, but he still feels that a friendship had grown between Walt and him since his wife's death. He sees the inheritance as a symbol of friendship and mutual acceptance despite all their differences. Walt's redemption through self-sacrifice does not correspond to the Christian idea of atonement and forgiveness, but he stayed true to his principle of self-reliance until his death. Walt left Thao more than his Gran Torino. The car was part of Walt and now lives on in Thao. Similarly, Walt treated Thao like a son, and passed on skills and values to him. These have turned Thao into a more self-confident young man with a brighter future. Walt sacrificed his own life to give the Van Lors a chance to live theirs in peace. By ending his own life, Walt could yet again follow his principles of self-reliance and self-determination. He was fatally ill – instead of losing his strength and dignity in a fight against illness, he stayed in control and decided for himself. He wanted peace for others and he found peace for himself.

IV   Bibliografie

Allgemein

Bradley, Martin (2013). *Teaching with Film. Bring the World into your Classroom. 136 Scenes from 100 Movies to integrate into your English Lessons.* Wien: Stone River.

Donaghy, Kieran (2015). *Film in Action. Teaching Language using Moving Images.* Delta Publishing.

Einhoff, Katharina (Hrsg.) (2011). *Power Pack English. Media Literacy – Practising Listening and Viewing Skills (Sek. II).* Braunschweig: Schöningh.

Sam B. Girgus (2014). *Clint Eastwood's America (America through the lens).* Polity.

Henseler, Roswitha et al. (2011). *Filme im Englischunterricht. Grundlagen, Methoden, Genres.* Klett/Kallmeyer.

McClelland, Richard T. and Brian B. Clayton (2014). *The Philosophy of Clint Eastwood.* University Press of Kentucky.

Ryan, Michael und Lenos, Melissa (2012). *An Introduction to Film Analysis. Technique and Meaning in Narrative Film.* New York: Continuum.

Suhrkamp, Carola (2010). *Close-up. Exploring the Language of Film.* Braunschweig: Schöningh. [Lernsoftware]

Thaler, Engelbert (2014). *Teaching English with Films.* Paderborn: Schöningh. Themenheft „Filme sehen – Filme verstehen" – *Der Fremdsprachliche Unterricht Englisch,* (112/113). 2011.

Filmkritiken und Artikel

Bradshaw, Peter (2009). *Gran Torino.* The Guardian, Feb 2009

Dargis, Manohla (2008). *Hope for a Racist, and Maybe a Country.* New York Times, Dec 2012

Davis, Adrienne D. (2009). *Intimacy in ‚Star Trek' and ‚Gran Torino'* http://papers.ssrn.com/sol3/papers.cfm?abstract_id=1571713

Foley, Philip (2009). *Gran Torino - Clint Eastwood Interview.* http://www.indielondon.co.uk/Film-Review/gran-torino-clint-eastwood-interview

French, Philip (2009). *Gran Torino.* The Guardian, Feb 2009

Levy, Emmanuel (2009). *Gran Torino: Interview with Clint Eastwood.* http://emanuellevy.com/comment/gran-torino-interview-with-clint-eastwood-2/

Luis-Lopez, Raul (2015). *Racism and Stereotype Review. Clint Eastwood's Gran Torino.* https://prezi.com/scwkgfdguzdo/gran-torino/

Machuco, Antonio (2010). *Violence and truth in Clint Eastwood's Gran Torino. UCLA* http://www.anthropoetics.ucla.edu/ap1602/1602machuco.htm

Romney, Jonathan (2009). *Gran Torino, Clint Eastwood,* The Independent, Feb 2009

Schein, Louisa (2010). *Gran Torino's Hmong lead Bee Vang on Film, Race and Masculinity: Conversations with Louisa Schein.* Hmong Studies Journal, Volume 11. http://hmongstudies.org/ScheinVangHSJ11.pdf

Weiß, Harald (2013). *Erlösung und Gerechtigkeit – allein in mir, allein im Hier. Religionskritisches und Medienreligiöses in den Filmen Clint Eastwoods.* http://www.theomag.de/85/hawe1.htm

Film & Material

Film script

http://www.imsdb.com/scripts/Gran-Torino.html

http://www.springfieldspringfield.co.uk/movie_script.php?movie=gran-torino

Trailer (englisch)

https://www.youtube.com/watch?v=RMhbr2XQblk

Original Theme Song

https://www.youtube.com/watch?v=MItMDkc343M

Original Movie posters

http://www.impawards.com/2008/posters/gran_torino_xlg.jpg

https://mir-s3-cdn-cf.behance.net/project_modules/disp/4f92c152175661.5608d24d8
b05c.png

http://www.eatbrie.com/large_posters_files/Grantorino3.jpg

https://www.cinematerial.com/media/posters/md/3g/3g16pwpy.jpg?v=1456683752

https://www.cinematerial.com/media/posters/md/kt/kt7ohuuz.jpg?v=1456306829

Alternative posters

https://alternativemovieposters.com/wp-content/uploads/2013/07/torinobg.jpg

http://pre08.deviantart.net/3b10/th/pre/f/2010/280/4/e/gran_torino_movie_
poster_by_papagaaislaai-d308pzt.jpg

http://www.popoptiq.com/wp-content/uploads/2013/12/tumblr_
my2eycYj311qzdglao1_500.jpg

Hintergrundinformation

Gran Torino film locations

http://www.movie-locations.com/movies/g/GranTorino.html#.V8gKjq7BEy4

Fakten und Hintergründe zum Film 'Gran Torino'

http://www.kino.de/film/gran-torino-2008/news/fakten-und-hintergruende-zum-
film-gran-torino/

Warner Bros. site

http://wwws.warnerbros.co.uk/grantorino/

Interview with Clint Eastwood on Gran Torino

https://www.youtube.com/watch?v=jXriv3tzXpw

Interview with Jamie Cullum

https://www.youtube.com/watch?v=01gOfBQ3Y78

Documentary: The Hmong (Two Parts)

https://www.youtube.com/watch?v=cy_yHyq-ZxU

https://www.youtube.com/watch?v=xC2zoxES45U

Video with 170 Greatest Clint Eastwood Movie Quotes

https://www.youtube.com/watch?v=K1vZq3bTS_Y

**Eine noch ausführlichere Bibliografie und Linksliste gibt es
über Klett-Online-Link: 935r64x**